Purposely Living on Cloud 9: Medicine for the Soul

Brisha Brichelle

ISBN 978-0615772974

Let's Get High!!! and Never Come Down!!! Purposely Living on Cloud 9 Getting the Whole World High.... One Book At A Time

Below is my favorite Bible Scripture translated in four different versions.

Jeremiah (33:3) ERV

Judah, pray to me, and I will answer you. I will tell you important secrets. You have never heard these things before.

Jeremiah (33:3) KJV

Call to me, and I will answer thee, and shew thee great and mighty things, which thou knowest not.

Jeremiah (33:3) NIV

Call to me and I will answer you and tell you great and unsearchable things you do not know.

Jeremiah (33:3) CPDV

Cry out to me and I will keep you. I will announce to you, great things, things that are certain, though you do not know them.

He said that he will answer you! GOD cannot tell a lie. The question is "Will you know how to hear his reply?" Will you recognize how he's responding to you? My hope is, that he has used this little blue book to simplify things...

"Your Life should be full of purpose!!! passion!!! & power!!!" ~Brisha Brichelle

Contents

Preface:

Why I Wrote This Book

Nothing in life happens by accident. You have to believe that with your whole heart—not excluding anything, especially this book in your hand or this CD playing, is a prime example of entering into a *purposed* realm of living.

—Brisha Brichelle

I had arrived at a pivotal point in my life that had led me to believe that my world was crashing down around me. It felt like the end of the world, but what I didn't realize was that it was the beginning of a *whole new world*. This book was not intended to be an autobiography, and it's not. I do plan to write a very detailed autobiography one day. However, it is very important that I give you a brief overview of the traumas, tragedies, and obstacles that I've overcome and still choose to be high on life, love, and happiness and all that they have to offer.

You must know why I've earned the right to believe, the right to know, as well as the right to tell you that you, too, can purposely live on Cloud 9, regardless of any and every thing that you may have encountered in your life thus far. Therefore, I do use my life's experiences as proof that, no matter what you go through, you can live purposely on Cloud 9 if you choose to.

Shortly after I was born, I was diagnosed with a terrible strand of meningitis. The prognosis that the doctors gave my parents was that my chances of recovery were only 50-50. That is, there was a 50 percent chance that I would have a debilitating deformity for the rest of my life, or a 50 percent chance that I would become extraordinarily smart, a genius of sorts. I do not have a physical deformity as result of the meningitis, and, of course, I'd love to consider myself a genius. However, I am not.

I would be lying if I said I've never wondered about all the *what ifs?*—such as, "What if I were suffering from a debilitating deformity? Who would be taking care of me?" Or "What if I were a genius? What would my life be like right now? Would I care about humanity as much as I do now?" I'm sure there are millions of *what *if* scenarios I could use. But that would contradict my statement that nothing in life happens by accident, wouldn't it?

As odd as this may sound, even an accident is not *by accident*. An accident is perceived as an accident the instant it happens, because it is an unexpected occurrence at that particular moment. However, once the accident is evaluated and understood, you realize its purpose. I know that everything has a purpose. Even what I'm doing right now, and what you're doing right now, has a purpose. It's how we *receive* the purpose that determines our understanding.

This beautiful opportunity to be the vessel chosen to write what I've written is one of the most honorable opportunities I've had in my life. I *know* that, although written by me, the words in this book permeated my spirit and took on a life of their own. Even while I was writing, I could feel my own spirit being continuously healed in areas where I myself am still growing.

I also know that to have this book edited by Paul Weisser and every other necessary step was all part of this book's profound purpose for the world. The most important part of this book was to have it read by *you*. If you internalize this book as I have, it will take you to an indescribable understanding of your life and everyone in it, as well as of all that has happened or will happen in your life.

This book will attract everyone who desires to live purposely on Cloud 9, even if you're unaware of that desire. It's your season. It's your time. Get ready for a complete understanding of your life and its purpose. This book was not just written; it was *born* to serve a powerful purpose in the world right now, and I'm so glad that *we* are part of the plan. I'm honored by this opportunity to write what I've written for your reading or listening enlightenment. Let's begin.

Most of my earliest memories of my dad are fun and happy. But I also remember that he used drugs on a regular basis. His drug of choice was crack cocaine. Although he loved my mother very much, he was also physically abusive to her from time to time. My parents separated when I was seven and my brother, Charles (or C.J.), was an infant. I remember my mother dating, and then moving us in to live with one man in particular—a known local hustler and full-time gambler. He was also extremely jealous of my mother's relationships with her family members, as well as any other person who would take her attention away from him, not excluding her children.

I can remember sneaking into the refrigerator one morning,

6

thinking that no one could see me, and attempting to drink water straight out of a jug without using a glass. However, the boyfriend caught me and, instead of telling me to stop or taking the jug a away from me, slapped me with an open palm on the side of my face, knocking me forward into the open refrigerator. I fell on all the shelves, which tumbled down to the floor—as I did.

I can recall another time when C.J. and I were jumping on the bed we shared. My back was turned and I was in mid-jump when I heard my little brother scream. As I turned around and nervously plopped down, I saw the boyfriend standing beside the bed with a belt in his hand, buckle side down. He had hit my brother, not me, this time. I don't know if the realization that he had just hit a two-year-old child in the head with a belt buckle stopped him from hitting me, but my mother came running into the room screaming, and yelled even louder when she saw the blood streaming down my brother's face. To this day, my brother has a scar on the crown of his head that I used to tell him came from a spider bite. It's only been in recent years that I've told him the true story.

Those are just two of many incidents when our mother threatened to leave the boyfriend, but was understandably afraid of him. I can still see him holding a 45mm gun to her head as he shouted, "Bitch, if you ever leave me, I'll blow your mutha%@!*$# brains out!"

Please excuse the explicit language, but imagine those words ringing in the ears of a young girl, watching her mother being threatened.

My mother was murdered on August 14, 1981, with a gunshot to her cheek, which blew her brain out and caused her to asphyxiate on her own blood. I was nine, and C.J. was two. Believe it or not, to this day no one has been prosecuted for the murder. However, I completely forgive my mother's murderer, whoever he (or she) may be, because I know that no one in his *right mind* would commit murder and leave two children motherless. Besides, I would not want to take anyone's parent or grandparent away, especially if the person has forgiven himself and is living a productive life. Who am I to judge? However, if the murderer has become a menace to society, I don't have an opinion about the matter. That should be between that individual and the justice system.

C.J. and I moved in with an aunt. I was very happy to be with her and her children, my cousins. My aunt had a live-in boyfriend, who was the first of many of my molesters. After months of him sneaking into my room and touching me, I found the strength to "tell on him." Although that caused a family uproar, it was never reported to the authorities. To this day, because he never touched anyone else in my family, I'm not even sure if anyone believes what happened to me. But that's okay. I'd rather it be this way than have him hurting my cousins, just to validate my story.

My dad took C.J. and me to live with him in his drug-infested apartment. I remember wishing I had never told anyone about the molestation, so I could still be living with my cousins.

My father had people coming in and out of the apartment all the time, using drugs. One of the men at one of those drug parties touched me very inappropriately, but I was afraid to tell anyone because I had no idea where we would go next. What I did do, whenever those people came over, was get my little brother and gather whatever food I could find in the kitchen and hide with him in the bedroom closet. I had food, a flashlight, and one *ET* movie poster. I would sit my brother on my lap, shine the flashlight on the poster, and make up stories about any and every detail in the poster. I would do that for hours to keep his attention until he fell asleep, and then I would cry myself to sleep.

My brother is incarcerated at this time, and in all honesty I feel that the lifestyle I exposed him to had a lot to do with the decisions he made to hang around with a certain type of people who may have caused him to end up in twisted situations. When I visited him one time in prison, he said to me that he had seen *ET* recently, but the only part he could remember was the bicycle ride. It was then that I informed him that I wasn't sure if he had ever seen the movie. Tears began to well up in my eyes when I explained to him what I did for us to keep us safe as children.

When we would wake up and come out of the closet, on some days there would be people sleeping all over the place. At other times, there would just be our father, sluggishly laid out wherever he had fallen. I remember finding syringes in the bathroom, throwing them away, and cleaning up whatever else was left, just to keep C.J. from getting into it.

On one particular day, my maternal grandmother came over to bring me clothes for school. When she saw the conditions we were living in, she convinced my father to let her take us with her. Not long after that, she had a stroke, and it wasn't long before she died. She was buried on July 24, 1984, my twelfth birthday.

C.J. suffered from asthma, and had an extremely difficult time breathing on the day of the funeral. A family member gave me some money for my birthday, so before the funeral service, I ran to the corner store to buy some medicine that I had seen advertised on TV for asthma.

"Oh, my God!" you might say. "This is a lot for two young children." Believe me, there is more.

My brother and I next moved in with an uncle and aunt. As the little woman I imagined myself to be, I attempted to cook myself some bacon for breakfast one morning—something I had done several times before. But this time I decided to pull a barstool close to the stove and cook while sitting on it. Unfortunately, I *accidentally* bumped my elbow against the handle of the pan, causing the hot grease to flip directly onto my lap. That gave me third-degree burns and a lifetime of insecurity.

I loved living in my aunt and uncle's home, but—probably because I didn't like being obedient—I would talk to my father on the phone frequently, and he would say that his children belonged with him. "Just take the bus," he said. And so, after about a year, I took C.J. to my paternal grandmother's house, where my father lived.

My dad later moved across the street from my grandmother, and we moved with him.

His drug habits hadn't changed. They may have actually intensified. In one of his drug-induced states, he himself became one of my molesters. I was thirteen, and told one of my family members what my father had done to me. The family member said, "If you wasn't so damn fast, it probably wouldn't have happened. You need to get your fast ass somewhere and sit down."

But I forgive that relative for saying that. That kind of situation was traditionally swept under the rug, but I began to believe that I had caused each one of those men to invade my space. I believed that it was my fault that I had brought this on myself, which led to a lifetime of sexual insecurities and relationship issues.

Next we went back to the maternal side of my family, living from family member to family member. I often burned my bridges along the way, because of my disobedience, and ended up running away, leaving C.J. with an aunt. By age fifteen, I was homeless and living from friend to friend. At some point, I figured that there was absolutely no reason for me to be alive. No one knew it, but I had already planned my exit. I was going to commit suicide!

I called a friend to pick me up, to take me to a different friend's house. The second friend's mother had a gun, and I knew exactly where it was, and couldn't wait to get to it. But my driving friend had an appointment first, so I ended up going to Planned Parenthood with her to get condoms. The clerk insisted that I get some too, and so did my friend. I remember thinking that they were wasting their time and mine, since they didn't know what I was planning to do, and I didn't want them to know. Therefore, I followed through with taking the stupid pregnancy test and receiving the pregnancy prevention package. If that speeds things up, I thought, so be it.

But it was then that I found out that I was pregnant at sixteen. I couldn't kill myself and the child, so the pregnancy saved my life. It also not only gave me someone to love, but someone who would love me. (I don't advocate teen pregnancy, but this situation was special.) So I had a son at seventeen, whose father was murdered when I was twenty-one. I began to live a very promiscuous life, but because I did not know what real love is, I did not know *how* to love—which caused me to get caught up with and be attracted to all the wrong men.

When I was twenty-five, in 1997, I met a man and married him two years later. I had a son, he had a daughter and a son, and we proceeded to have a son together, so we had a total of four children between us.

Meanwhile, I had survived the incident with my dad, and so long as he wasn't high in my presence, I saw past his flaws and appreciated his efforts to be the best father he knew how to be. It was comforting to know that I at least had one of my parents. However, my father died of a drug overdose in 2007.

There were great times during my marriage, but we struggled with combining the families, among many other issues, and after twelve years, the marriage ended in divorce in 2011. I believe that those fourteen years of marriage gave me the only sense of stability that I've known in my entire life, even though the marriage wasn't perfect. It was during that time that I had the opportunity to adjust to some sense of normality.

In any case, going through a divorce was not solely about the divorce, because it caused every tragic experience from my past to come back to haunt me. My life began to gnaw at whatever sense of sanity I thought I had. How I would survive emotionally I had no idea. But what I knew was that I had to be strong—not just for myself but for my two children. I remember crawling on the floor, screaming without any sound coming from my mouth. My soul was in pain. And the most fearful part about it all was the realization that I was completely alone again, without anyone to turn to.

There were a few family members and friends who reached out to me. Without one very close cousin in particular, Anissa, it would have been an even more tragic experience to overcome. Yet and still, that was the emptiest I had felt in a very long time.

Now you have an overview of some of the major calamities in my life, and yet I still choose to have a joyful and purposeful life. As you read further, you will not only understand why, but how.

Something very profound happened to me on December 31, 2010, at the Potter's House Church in Dallas, Texas. It was the Watch Night service, a New Year's Eve celebration in the black community. I remember being slain in the spirit, with my arms spread wide open, constantly repeating the word *yes!* with tears streaming down my face. Yes, yes, yes! I had no idea of the true meaning of those *yes*'s! I knew I was excited, and I assumed that my life was about to become perfect and extremely easy. But it was quite the contrary.

All *hell* broke loose in my home, three days later. My life, and the life of my entire family, was turned upside down forever. I had been a member of the Potter's House Church since 2007, a few months after my father's death left me spiritually detached. Although I had a terrible experience with my dad, I forgave him because I saw his love for family, his love for God, his love for Jesus Christ, and, most of all, his love for C.J. and me. And in my heart of hearts, I thought my dad was going to be delivered from drugs and be here with C.J. and me forever. We all think that of our parents. So his death came as a shock, and I was broken yet again.

That is when the teachings of Bishop TD Jakes and my alone time in the presence of God began to allow me to see God's hand in everything I experienced, including in everything that I had lost. I began to understand the purpose for everything and everybody in my life, and I developed a prolific understanding of the people and things that were no longer in my life, for whatever reason. What was so extraordinary for me was that it seemed as if every single message that was preached every single Sunday of 2011, whether it was preached by Bishop TD Jakes or a guest pastor, was designed just for me. (God's word is so amazing that in a church of more than 30,000 souls, we all feel the same way.) I knew I was in divine alignment with what God was trying to do in me, to me, and through me. My purpose was miraculously being revealed to me.

It took me forty years to figure everything out. Or should I say, for God to get my *attention*? It is now my honor to pass along information that will enlighten you, in a much shorter time than it took to enlighten me, and to allow you the ability to have peace, joy, and happiness, not only in the great times of your life, but in the most tragic and trying times as well. I hope that I reflect not only the light of my Lord and Savior Jesus Christ, but also the wonderful teachings that were deposited in me by my pastor and spiritual father. It is my honor to share what I have learned and experienced, with the hope that I can help you to reach Cloud 9.

The beautiful thing is that I know this book will reach everyone that it's supposed to reach. This is a *purposed* book, so if it is in your hand, *know* that you are on purpose and on course. Look around, see where you are, where you're sitting or standing, and absorb the moment. This is your *epiphanic* moment, if I may coin a word.

Better yet, grab a pen, a cell phone, a tablet, or whatever you use for record-keeping, and write down exactly what you are doing as you begin to purposely live on Cloud 9.

Today is the day that you began to intentionally live your life on purpose, regardless of how imperfect you may think your life has been. Everyone has a story, each of which is unique, like fingerprints. Your story is extremely important. *You* are important. That is why it is necessary for you to begin to live the life you were created to live. You may not choose to be as transparent as I am, but it is in my transparency that I have the ability to help you to recognize and process painful truths. It doesn't matter how your life began. What matters is how you live and how your life ends. You have the opportunity right now to turn your life around so that it is happy and meaningful.

Chapter 1:

In the Beginning…

It is by no accident that this information is in your hand, and you're reading it right now. Believe it or not, you have attracted this book to you. Once you've become aware that life does not just happen, then you will understand that everything you do, see, or experience is a huge contributing factor to your purpose on Earth.

Your birth was no accident, even if it was unplanned. The accident may have been in the act, but not in the conception of the child. Only God can breathe life—contrary to what most scientists believe, as well as those who perceive themselves as highly intelligent or elitist. This book is clearly for you. It's extraordinarily simple and easy to understand, and therefore very digestible.

I intend nothing less than to prove the evidence of God from my own personal experiences, which are based on faith—which is the substance of things hoped for, the evidence of things not seen.

There are people who believe that religion is a crutch, I don't have a total argument against that, actually. Personally, I consider it an amazing opportunity to lean on God's unfailing love. And what's so beautiful is that God understands and forgives even those who cannot understand his omniscience presence throughout the universe. Therefore, it is written, forgive them for they know not. God loves you even when you could not care less about him.

The good news is that there will come a time when even the biggest nonbelievers will believe. For example, according to a story reported in the *Huffington Post*, a former atheist named Patrick Greene threatened to sue the city of Athens, Texas, over a nativity scene in front of the courthouse. But then he fell ill, and despite his previous actions against Christianity, church members in town came together to raise funds for his family. Greene last reported that he had become a Christian and wanted to enter the ministry to gain a better understanding of his new faith.

There are thousands of stories like Greene's that speak of transformation. This book was written to help you to live in internal peace on purpose. Therefore, what you do with the knowledge received from this book will be up to you. However, I strongly encourage you to apply it piece by piece to your daily life. When you do this, you will realize that no one and nothing can change your new level of conscious living, if you allow the words in this book to nourish your soul, your being, and your thoughts.

Starting today, you will begin to spend the rest of your life purposely living on Cloud 9. That does not mean that your life will become perfect. We all know that there is no one on Earth who lives a perfect life. However, what it does mean is that you will begin to truly appreciate the life that you've been given and to purposefully live it, accepting everything that has ever happened to you, appreciating everything you are, and understanding all that you are not.

By the end of this book, you will be excited about you newly found perception of life. Most importantly, you will have developed the ability to understand that everything that has happened, is happening, or will happen in your life has purpose and meaning, even if it is terribly painful. When you consistently apply the nuggets from this book, understanding that purpose, will be easy for you to do, even when you're facing tragedies, trauma, and life-changing situations. You will have also developed the keen ability to truly appreciate all things great while they are happening to you. This skill is very important, because you will not run the risk of forfeiting those great opportunities, which most people usually lose because they do not value what they have while they have it. It is only when they are gone that they realize what they had was great.

You're going to learn how to avoid this problem. This book will not only give you the ability to grasp your greatness, but you will also be able to recognize the unusual gifts and people that miraculously appear in your life because of your new depth of recognition. The gift of being able to recognize before loss is not to be taken lightly. When you have developed this gift, you will recognize and appreciate things that are already in your life. This will include people who are already in your life that you may have been overlooking, simply because you did not know how to recognize or appreciate them.

By reading this book, you will have been exposed to necessary information, not only to harness these gifts but how to display the utmost admiration for those gifts. You will appreciate the life that you have been allowed to live, the people that you have been allowed to know, and the experiences that you have been allowed to have, because they are just that—gifts. This appreciation will cause you to receive more gifts because it's the law---whatever you give you get. Besides everyone loves to be appreciated, whether they tell you or not. Even God loves to be appreciated and praised.

You must be able to be trusted with the gifts that you are given. This book is going to teach you how to be trusted with your Blessings, so that you will maintain them. This book covers gratitude and its affect on everything that you are. It teaches how applying gratitude will elevate your life. All by itself, the conscious act of showing gratefulness will attract everything you need in your life.

Choosing not to apply the content in this book will only prolong your opportunity to begin living the purposeful life that is rightfully yours. You do deserve the desires of your heart, don't you? Of course, you do. Otherwise, they would not be your desires. How you handle what you receive throughout your life is what determines how long you will have it in your life. Consequently, it will be only your fault if you do not allow the words in this book to elevate you immediately.

If I could etch every word in this book into your brain, I would. But I cannot. Nor can I make you read any further. I am so very grateful that you're reading this book. For some of you, this may be the first book that you have read a book in a while. For others, this may be a part of your constant quest to find meaning and purpose.

I believe that this book contains exactly the right words to take you to a state of blissful living. I know that this book is something that your soul yearns for. Your desire to know your purpose and exactly who you are is why you're still reading. You're getting closer and closer, word by word, to knowing just that.

It is time to introduce the real you to the world, rather than the impersonator that even you sometimes may not know. It is time to remove the mask and get behind your façade. It is finally time for you to be and to enjoy exactly who you are. This book will help you to do precisely that. You must change from within. The good news is that this book ignites that burning desire to be all that you are created to be and to consciously live on Cloud 9.

I cannot insist that you consider me the most valuable source of information. There is information everywhere, and I suggest that, after finishing this book, you continue to read books that uplift, motivate, and inspire you to continue cultivating your being.

But right now, you're here with me, and I want to captivate you in every moment I have with you. I'm so very grateful that you are here with me. I prayed for you, and every other person that will read or listen to this book. I pray that God fulfills every desire of your heart that you gain a permanent focus. I made a promise to share my experience of blissful living with the world and be completely transparent about it. Doing so has served as such a healing, not just for myself but for a vast number of others. Achieving a Cloud 9 level of living was the most amazing accomplishment in my life. That is why I am sharing it. Everyone deserves to reach a level of love, peace and understanding of yourself and everything around you. It will give you a sense of euphoria that never leaves you.

Most of all, I give my love, in the hope that you will see past every obstacle and distraction, including anything and everyone who may have caused you harm in the past. I pray that you will be able to recognize your place and how valuable you are on this Earth. The time is now for you to begin to live your life purposefully.

There are multitudes of people who speak, teach, and write the exact words needed to put us back together again, or help us to find our purpose in life. That is why we read books like this one, attend churches, seek counseling, or see a therapist. I know that from experience because it was in my own brokenness that I sought refuge in those places. Everyone is looking for an answer to the ultimate question Why am I here? Not only did I receive clear answers while I prayed to my heavenly father, but also while I listened in church to my Bishop. I also received encouragement from friends, associates, and books. I sought to make myself better in the midst of almost losing my sanity. I refused to allow the enemy to inundate my mind with failure and hopelessness.

I was born to do exactly what I'm doing now: assisting others with finding inner peace, joy, and happiness. That is why I dealt with multiple tragic experiences throughout my life. Even in the midst of my traumatic experiences, I still found myself encouraging others, although not as much as I can do now. There were phases in my life that I would let the next tragedy hinder me for years at a time before

I could slowly begin my purposeful life. It was during those unhappy times that I had no clue how to maintain my own joy. As a result, I would lose my sense of self, little by little in every devastating situation.

It was not until I experienced my very own ah-ha moment that the light bulb came on. That experience occurred during what I perceive now as having been on the brink of a total shutdown. It was either give up or get up. I am not a quitter. So I got up and began the fight for my life. I had to take life by the horns and ride it like a bull. Purposely living on Cloud 9 became a part of my fiber, regardless of the situations. Now I understand exactly how to remain on Cloud 9, no matter curve of life I'm in.

One of my many assignments in this world is to share this information with others. It is definitely a key to living—if not the master key. This is definitely information that will do me no good at all if I keep it to myself. I am so excited to be sharing with you right now. My prayer is that I have formulated a goulash of sorts that may never win a Nobel Peace Prize, but will give thousands, if not millions, peace. PEACE is a prize within itself.

This book will repeat certain points because repetition is a key to understanding. It is very important that you understand everything that is repeated. Allow the words to be internalized and brought to life, not just read. Even if your life is amazing right now, there's always something more to learn until the day you stop breathing. Everyone is all too aware that the storms of life will come. No matter how rich, religious, or smart you are, you will be subject to misfortune in your lifetime. So I know that this book is not only a necessary key to assisting you right now, but also in the future, when you will be faced with situations that seem hopeless.

This book was written to ignite as well as reignite your fire at any point in time when you need it. Please allow it to be medicine for your soul. So I say thank you in advance from the core of my heart for allowing me to assist you in blissful living for as long as you live. This book is intended for everyone everywhere. Whether you are in the United States or a foreign country. Whether you are homeless or living in a penthouse. Whether you are a construction worker or the CEO of a Fortune 500 company. Whether you are institutionalized mentally or physically. Everyone deserve the life of their dreams, and that starts with knowing how to live purposely on Cloud 9.

My prayer is that you will not only read this book, but inhale it into your psyche. I want you to receive its wisdom into your being to initialize a transformation as long as you stay consciously aware of yourself. You can do this by understanding and applying the contents of this book to every day of your life. Purposely living on Cloud 9 will be as immediate as you allow it to be. As soon as you begin to live your life on purpose, the process will begin to work. Therefore, I am completely assured that you are in for an excellent reading or listening experience. The secret is that everyone has a chance for a do-over. And it can begin right now.

I am completely certain that if you consciously choose to live purposely, you will be living on Cloud 9 forever. Please join me on Cloud 9. There is room for everyone who chooses to relocate to a complete life of daily purposeful living.

Chapter 2:
Recognizing Your Dysfunctions and Working Through Them

Your birth was the beginning of your purposeful living. Your exact date and time of birth were the beginning of your purpose. The exact parents that you were born through is exactly how it was supposed to be—whether they were perceived by you as perfect or not. Whether or not your parents were in your life, you have to realize that your life has purpose.

You must also be aware that you have to come to grips with who you are, in order to begin to understand your purpose. You have to understand who you are and why you do the things you do. You must come to grips with why you react negatively to some situations and why you are unable to maintain lasting friendships, relationships, and jobs. The primary reason for all of this is dysfunction, whether you are aware of it or not. You have to understand that life happens, for good or for bad. And if you have never learned how to embrace life's changes, they can cripple you forever, causing an eternal downward dysfunctional spiral. Believe it or not, everyone has some form of dysfunction to some extent. The ability to begin to recognize your dysfunctions is what allows you to harness the necessary information to rise above your weaknesses.

To overcome a dysfunction, you must admit to yourself that there are areas in your life that need to be healed, most likely from early childhood experiences. Family dysfunction is usually generational and hereditary if the cycle is not broken. However, even the strongest families go through periods of functional impairment, such as when parents are irresponsible, or a family member abuses drugs, or someone becomes ill or dies.

However, what "healthy" families have is the ability to recover because they seek proper professional help. The faster you seek help, the faster you or your family members can begin to recover from dysfunction. What happens in "unhealthy" families is that they do not seek help, and thus begin to function in their *dys*function, thereby creating lifelong problems.

You may not even be aware of your dysfunction, because it is all you know, so you have become accustomed to your handicaps. These serious dysfunctional weaknesses are severely crippling to the development of your children, because you pass them on without realizing it, since they are part of your everyday experience.

Let's go through a few dysfunctions and begin to identify them, so that you can begin your journey to purposely live on Cloud 9 with complete understanding.

You probably have a dysfunction:
- if as a child you did not get most of your needs met.
- if you were raised in an abusive family.
- if you were abandoned.
- if you never felt a sense of belonging.
- if you experienced early childhood trauma.
- if you had alcoholic or drug-abusing parents.
- if you experienced excessive yelling, screaming, cursing, and anger as a child.
- if you never received the proper healthy attention.
- if you experienced many broken promises.
- if you were sexually abused.
- if you were raised in an unstable environment.
- if you were not allowed to have individuality.
- if you were a latchkey kid.
- if you had to be an adult much earlier than most

other children.
- if you were belittled or criticized.

This is just to name a few dysfunctions. Many of them will leave you feeling powerless, inadequate, frustrated, and even angry at times—especially if you have no idea where the frustration or anger came from. I am a firm believer in the old saying that if you spare the rod, you spoil the child, meaning that corporal punishment is sometimes necessary. Of course, this varies with the child, and there should never be fractures, bleeding, or bruises. That is clearly physical abuse.

There are many signs that you may have come from a dysfunctional family, or that you are a dysfunctional adult trying to appear as functional as possible, while feeling helpless or hopeless in your heart. Feelings of unworthiness and shame may continue to surface because of early childhood experiences. There is no need to be embarrassed by this. It is the embarrassment that traps you in the dysfunction. There are more people who are clinically dysfunctional than you may imagine.

I learned to function in my dysfunction and mask its crippling effects in my life. At least, that's what I thought. I tried to function normally in dysfunction, not realizing that there is nothing normal about dysfunction. As soon as I became aware of the problem, I got busy addressing the issues. I began to deal with each childhood devastation, no matter how painful it was. I had to face the fact that I was broken, bruised, abused, misused, and hurt. But none of that defined who I was or what I was to become. I no longer felt the need to appear as if I had it all together. I began to nurture my broken self, receive counseling, and study the word of God. Most importantly, I accepted myself for who I am. Then I could begin my functional life with an understanding that I am a work in progress.

We are all a continued work in progress until the day we die, and we must recognize that in order to have a productive, functional life. You must understand that nothing in your childhood is your fault. You were a child, even if you were disobedient and unruly. There was an initial trigger to the onset of this behavior. Thus began your dysfunction, even if it went unrecognized for your entire life. If you do not have the ability to understand or recognize the cause of the dysfunction, or you simply refuse to be honest with yourself, you will never be able to heal. You are only band-aiding the situation. And as we all know, band-aids are a temporary fix, but air is needed as well to heal the wound. You have to allow your issues to be aired out. Otherwise, you will fall deeper and deeper into cycles of dysfunctional situations because you have no idea who you are, what your purpose is, and what you're searching for.

Maybe you were raised in a single-parent home, and your mother had to be both mother and father. Maybe you were raised by both parents, but because of their lack of parenting skills, you have dysfunctional characteristics. They did what they could to the best of their ability. However, this created a dysfunctional child. They did not know how to show love. They assumed that being the providers was sufficient proof of their love. But not being affirmed as a child creates an insecure adult. And affirmation is critical even for adults. That is why it is so easy for young women and men to be victimized by predators offering a false sense of love, which causes them to think they're in love because they have filled a temporary void. Or we think it's love for physical reasons. When true love is at the core it is forever, and because you have now arrived at the point in your life that you're ready to get past the things that debilitated you and move forward into your purpose, you have unlocked a vital key to begin the healing of your dysfunction.

Not handling a dysfunction properly or addressing the issues behind it will cause you to spend your life searching for love in what appears to be a loveless world. I have news for you. The world is full of love—pure, genuine love—but in order to find it, you must first love yourself, regardless of whether or not you are being loved by someone else. Yes, when someone else loves you, that is great. But when you love yourself, you experience the greatest love of all.

You will learn to love people for who they are, and not for who you want them to be. You will realize that they are made up of their childhood experiences, which may or may not be causing the character they are presenting to you. You will find that you can love them without losing yourself, and—believe it or not—regardless of whether they are loving you back or not. Most often, it is the unconditional love you have for someone that allows that person to see God's love through you.

True love is unconditional, in spite of a person's dysfunction. You can learn to love, or at least how to love someone during their dysfunction. With the help of this book, you will not only be able to recognize and release your dysfunctions, but you will be able to assist countless others in the process as well. You are learning to love not only yourself, but people in general, the way God loves, unconditionally. Even the most unbearable people deserve love. The cycle *stops here!*

Chapter 3:
Breaking the Chains

First, accept and believe that nothing you experienced in your childhood was your fault. Recognize any and all of the dysfunctions that you have been carrying throughout your life. Those dysfunctions no longer have control over you, because you have recognized them. You now have the ability to free yourself from them, as well as free yourself from others who have tried to control you through your dysfunctions. Forgive yourself *right now!*

The mistakes you made in your past, no matter what they are, do not determine what you will do from this moment on. Whether you are a doctor, a corporate executive, a music industry professional, a beautician, a prisoner, a housewife, an exotic dancer, an engineer, a nurse, a truck driver, a billionaire, or a homeless person, no one is perfect.

We have all made our fair share of mistakes, and as long as we exist on this planet, we will continue to make them. It is the ability to recognize that you have made a mistake that earns you the right to receive your do-over. So forgive those who may have hurt you in any way. Forgiving them frees you. What I really want you to understand is that, in forgiving others, you recognize them, not as your perpetrator, but as human beings. These people were once someone's small children. They did not receive the necessary help to prevent them from hurting within themselves later in their life. One of the hardest things a person can deal with is overcoming sexual dysfunction. Most of these dysfunctions are brought on by the innocence of a child being robbed very early in life. I speak on this from experience. It's even more difficult for a man to overcome childhood dysfunctions from molestation. There is a haunting memory that destroys beyond the years of the act. These dysfunctions can definitely play a part in your life as an adult, making it difficult to maintain meaningful relationships. Oftentimes people do not share with their spouses the things that happened to them early in their lives, for fear of how they will be perceived. A man in particular may be viewed as homosexual.

For me, even though I had lost my physical virginity, I was never emotionally connected sexually. Because of my sexual dysfunctions, I never had the opportunity to experience intimacy for the beauty that it truly is. This is not to discredit any relationship that I've had in the past, but during those times I really had no idea who I was, so my physical involvement in the act was disconnected from my spirit. But when two souls truly connect physically and spiritually, in the midst of intimacy, I believe that's heaven on Earth.

The sooner you receive counseling, or begin to truly discover your purpose and quest in life, the sooner your connection to life and everything it has to offer will become as clear as crystal.

Prompt attention to sexual dysfunction is extremely beneficial to any relationship. Completely forgive the people who have hurt you in the past, even sexually, so they cannot continue to destroy your intimacy for the rest of your life. They do not deserve that right. Not only is it important to share this information with your mate, instead of keeping it to yourself, but if you make sure that your mate has a complete understanding of who you are, that will make for a better relationship. If openness and honesty end the relationship before it even gets started, that is not always a bad idea. It's either hurt now or hurt later. With honesty, both parties will know exactly who and what they are dealing with, and they can decide whether or not this is the type of relationship their character can support.

It is important to receive the help necessary to heal because you cannot have a healthy relationship unless you do. Get the necessary help, or even exposure to a book like this, that could have prevented them from hurting you—or anyone else.

Dysfunctions are just like children. Once you have them, they are there forever. In the early stages, you must bottle-feed them, change their diapers, and do everything else that comes with having a baby. Then they go off to elementary school, middle school, and high school, and maybe even college, and then they move out altogether and start their own families. But they are still yours, no matter how much time they require. Throughout the whole process, they are there. Just like dysfunctions, they belong to you as you heal them. As you choose friends and even lovers, know that all people have their fair share of dysfunction. It is up to you to decide what is tolerable.

I am pleased to offer this book to the world in the hope that people reading it will 'begin to nurse their dysfunctions. Discovering and healing your very own dysfunctions usually gives you the ability to see life with a whole new perspective. Break your chains right here and now!

In being negative, you bring negativity to yourself more intensely than the initial negativity you release. You've heard of gravity: what goes up must come down. And coming down is a lot faster than going up. Breaking your chains begins with releasing every negative thought from your mind forever. Is it possible not to have a negative thought ever again? Probably not. However, it is possible to be forever conscious of when you are being negative. So whatever comes out of your mouth, good or bad, will come back to you.

If you want to be responsible for something, why not be responsible for something good? That makes sense to me. Does it make sense to you? I'm quite sure it does, so for the rest of your life, be very careful of what you do and say, because everything comes back to you. I'm sure you've heard that before. Maybe not in those exact terms. Probably something like this: What goes around comes around. Or you reap what you sow All these phrases mean the same thing. Whatever you do to others, you do to yourself.

You may not see the effects immediately, but you will when you least expect them. Do not be alarmed. This proves true for the great things in your life as well. Relinquishing negativity brings forth an amazing life. Negativity will be in the world as long as people choose to function in it. But to break the chains of all dysfunctions, focusing on everything positive will create a life of blissful living.

In the middle of whatever it is you're going through, find the ability to have joy in the middle of madness. Ten percent of life is what happens to you, ninety percent is how you handle it. It's all about perception. I had a conversation with a friend, who told me that she felt bad because she had been married four times. I said to her, "It's all in how you look at it. You should be happy that you had the opportunity to experience falling in love four times. There are many people who have never experienced love at all, or ever been married, or had anyone who wanted to marry them even once."

My friend said, "I would be embarrassed to get married a fifth time. "It doesn't matter what anyone else thinks of you," I said. "You have to live with the decisions you make. At the end of the day, it's between you and your mate whether it's your fourth, fifth, sixth, or twentieth marriage."

I had a similar conversation with a cousin who has never been married. "How beautiful it is," I said, "to still be waiting for the perfect fit for the rest of your life." Again, it's all a matter of perception—how you perceive things to be. You can look at the negatives of any situation and intensify what is bad, or you can look at the positives of the situation and magnify the good. I refuse to view a glass as half-empty; it is always half-full. I urge you to adopt this way of thinking. Imprint it on your mind and say it every day.

The very thing that was designed to destroy you can lead you to your purpose. Research has proven that many of the skills and survival tactics that are a result of a dysfunctional childhood can become assets in adulthood. Researchers say that a child with a dysfunction develops a strong sense of survival at all costs. I believe that one hundred percent. In fact, I am living proof of it. Survival became my middle name.

It is also said that dysfunctional children develop a profound sense of empathy for others. There again I am guilty. I feel the need to help everybody in any way I can, and it never occurred to me until recently that this is a dysfunction. But I have to be honest: this is one dysfunction that I do not want to lose. I feel as though I am Dorothy in *The Wizard of Oz*, seeking help on the road and willing to bring everyone else along with me. The brainless scarecrow, the heartless tin man, the cowardly lion, and anybody else who needs to see Oz— including *you*.

On my quest, I realized that Oz is God. I believe that it is my purpose to help anyone everywhere as much as I can. If giving is my addiction, then I will gladly forever be an addict. No apologies here. I've been in situations in which I have helped people who have regarded me as gullible or naïve. In fact, that was not the case. I could see clearly through them into their dysfunction and had pity on them. I continued to help them anyway because so many people operate in their dysfunction for so long that they have become unaware of its presence. This is especially true of manipulative people. True healing from a dysfunction is not only being able to recognize it in yourself, but also in others, and still be able to tolerate them for their season in your life.

So be careful and guarded, yet mindful that being guarded does not mean being unapproachable. It means seeing things exactly as they are, but not always having to call them out, yet recognizing them in yourself and in others, and doing what you can to help all the parties involved.

You must control all of your emotions. Talk to friends, relatives, and even members of support groups to release your feelings. It is very important that you get them out. Nevertheless, I want you to understand that not everyone is going to care how you feel, and that's okay. To your surprise, there will be some people, or even a special person, who *will* care how you feel. When you find others who genuinely want to see you emotionally happy and healthy, cherish them and keep them close to you. They are few and far between.

I want to warn you that you will come across cruel people, who will attempt to use your weaknesses against you. Just remember that they are operating in their own dysfunctions, so simply release them and move on. Believe it or not, writing is a very sure way to release emotions. Try writing a letter to your enemies, or even to yourself, just to release the pain. Then shred the letter like Shredded Wheat. This will give you the release that is necessary to begin purposely living on Cloud 9.

Keep in mind that you and other people were allowed to cross paths so you could learn from each other, even in the worst of relationships. It is in those situations that I think about what Jesus must have thought when he said, "Forgive them, father, for they know not what they do." People sometimes do not know how helpful you could be to them and their lives if they would stop treating you the way they do. But that's not the point. It's time to realize what and who really matters to you. Do you know who you are? Do you know what your assignment on this Earth is? Do you know what you are capable of? You don't, do you? In the next chapter, you will have an *opportunity* to uncover your purpose.

Chapter 4:

The Journey of

Becoming You

Trying to function in life without knowing who you are, or your self-worth, or your value as a person, can cause you to live in a constant identity crisis. It is safe to say that your previous dysfunctions made you unable to truly know who you are. We usually spend a lifetime being who we are *not*—unless someone or something has caused us to look within ourselves and become who we actually are. It is only then that you can truly live your life on purpose. It is impossible to live someone else's dream or destiny.

Whatever is for *you* is *for* you. But at the same time, it is up to you to do whatever is necessary to discover those things for yourself. It is by no accident that you are about to discover who you are and what your purpose is. The time is now. The old saying rings true. Time waits for no one.

You can receive all of this information now, or put the book down and come back to it later where you left off. But why slow the process of a life of peace, joy, and success when it is waiting for you? All you have to do is reach out and grab it. It will be there, I promise. How do you do that? you ask.

Stand in front of a mirror, look deeply into your eyes, and say to yourself:

*** PERSONAL DECREE***

I am amazing. I am loved. It doesn't matter who loves me. I love me. I'm confident in who I am. I choose to live my life on purpose. I understand that this may not be easy, but I refuse to give up. I will fight for me and for you. I believe in us. We can do all things and anything that we put our minds to do. All goals are achievable. All unhealthy dysfunctions are removed. I am free regardless of who likes me. I will not be defined by others. I will be who I was purposed to be. And that is me. I will walk with my head high, even when the masses do not agree. I will stand for what I believe. I believe in me. Together we can and will live our life purposely on Cloud 9.

You just spoke to your spirit, and it heard and received every word. Now it is up to you to repeat this pledge to yourself every day. You can even write the words out and tape them to your mirror. Or keep them with you to serve as a reminder when you are discouraged.

You are no longer concerned with pleasing people. You must realize that you cannot please everybody all the time. It's impossible. So long as the reflection in the mirror is pleased with the decisions and choices you have made, you are on the right course.

It is not the materialistic things that make you who you are—not money and not success. If you have no sense of self when you obtain those things, you will still be empty and incomplete. Accept the fact that you are who you are. Everything about you is exactly how it should be. However, if there are areas in your life that you want to improve, take the necessary steps to grow. If you want to become a painter, take classes on painting. If your desire is to play the piano, take piano lessons. Whatever it is you desire, do that—so long as it doesn't hurt you or anyone else.

You must take the necessary steps to begin, for faith without works is dead. So get up, get out, and surround yourself with people who are moving in the direction you want to go. Appreciate everything in your past, because it made you exactly who you are. Transform the weaknesses of your past into the fuel for your future. Everything that happened to you in your past is just that—your past. There is absolutely nothing you can do about it now. Simply release the negative effect that it has on your life and focus on whatever positive came from it. If nothing positive came from it, then give it no attention at all.

During your self-discovery, it is very important that you allow yourself some time to be alone with yourself. This is when you go to your favorite place, whether it your bedroom, a fancy hotel in Hawaii, or your prayer closet. It is a place where you know you will not be disturbed. Take the opportunity to pray, meditate, and simply relax, allowing nothing to disturb this moment. Stay there as long as you like. Go there as often as you need. And it is fine if you cry. Whether you are a male or female, it is okay to cry. Tears do not show weakness; they exude strength and meekness. Tears are a great source of relief and release. They are cleansing, refreshing, and purifying.

This is your time. Use it however you wish. I like to talk to God and tell him how grateful I am for all that he's done in my life—and how grateful I am for you reading this book right now. I prayed in my secret closet that all the tragedies, traumas, stresses, pains, hurts, and abuses that I experienced in my life allowed me to orchestrate this book in such a way that it will help you to know that you are not alone, and that we as a people can get through any adversities.

I pray that your heart is softened enough to forgive yourself as well as anyone else who has hurt you. I also pray that you may begin to soar higher than you've ever soared before, so you can have peace and an amazing sense of self, allowing you to conquer the world. You can do all things through Christ that strengthen you. I ask God to breathe life into your visions, your dreams, and your thoughts in such a way that you are able to walk boldly and strongly and confidently in the new you.

This is a portion of what happens in my secret place. You can tell me and the world about *your* secret place by visiting this website:

You can share your transformation, your testimonials, or anything else you like. I look forward to hearing from you. My soul is so excited for you. Please visit often because it keeps you connected with like-minded people, enabling you to be a healthier, happier you.

One good exercise is uninhibited laughter. If you don't believe me, log on to YouTube, type in "funny pranks," and see if you do not begin to laugh uncontrollably. I do this often. If I feel a sense of sadness seeping in, laughter is always good for the soul. In fact, there was a study in which people watched Three Stooges movies, and blood was taken from them before, during, and after the viewing. Amazingly, the blood drawn while they were watching the movies and laughing contained chemicals that eat tumors!

Chapter 5:
Motivation Matters

Motivation is a necessary key to life. Not only is it important that you motivate yourself, but you must also motivate others. This book was written to encourage to do just that: to uplift, inspire, and motivate you. You can tell by the cover of the book that a lifting was going to take place here. On the cover, there are two images, both of which are silhouettes of me. What I'm implying on the cover is that you must motivate and encourage yourself, as well as others. Although people may assume that you should be perfect before you begin such a process, that is not true. There is a Chinese proverb that states that when someone shares something of value with you, and you benefit from it, you have a moral obligation to share it with others. This is why I am sharing what I've learned and experienced in my life. My prayer is that this book will quickly stimulate your mind in such a way that you become a permanent resident on Cloud 9.

There is purpose in every single person on the planet. Your decision in choosing to read this book implies that you are pursuing your purpose. Not only do I share my experiences with you here, but I also share research that I've done, in an attempt to prepare this book in such a way that you will eagerly apply these words daily. I have no idea how many people will read this book; however, I do know that there is power in numbers. And the more people who read this book and apply its truths, the bigger the impact will be on the world. What is important to me about this book is that I look forward to people feeling a strong sense of empowerment and triumph. I also look forward to the testimonials of chains being broken and dysfunctions being demolished.

I am not sharing my story to arouse your pity. Rather, I am sharing it to show that you can come from dysfunction and debilitation to purpose and bliss. The average person may look at my life and assume that I have no reason to be happy and so full of joy. To remain on Cloud 9 takes practice. You cannot allow people with negative energy to pull you down to their level. Some people will do this without thinking because your level of joy will look artificial to them, since the world has grown accustomed to constant confusion, chaos, trauma, and drama. Therefore, when you are always happy and full of joy, you run the risk of being perceived as over the top or unrealistic.

Let me tell you now, that is alright. You do not have to justify your happiness, any more than you need to allow someone to rob you of your happiness. You will have days of sadness, but that's okay. It does not mean that you are no longer on Cloud 9. When you are sad, it's okay to cry, if you don't cry too long. Don't focus on the bad things, give all your energy to what is good. Give no energy to what is bad—not even negative attention, because that is still attention. Surround yourself with positive people who do positive things. Stay close to those who encourage you.

I attend church regularly and read my Bible often because that is the most amazing motivational book on the planet; it is the source of all my strength, against all odds. When I say I have made it, I am not describing material success. I am describing a kind peace that surpasses all understanding. It is important to your well-being to allow positivity to flow into and out of you. I cannot reiterate enough that you reap what you sow. That is one of the reasons I wrote this book.

During church services, I have a heightened sense of self that I cannot describe. I always feel as if I can spread my arms and fly like an eagle because of my emotions, my adrenaline. My excitement reaches an indescribable euphoric plateau, and as soon as the service is over, I feel deflated and back to the real world. Well, guess what? It is your right to remain on the euphoric plateau for the rest of your life, and church as well as anything else should only enhance what you are capable of having continuously. It is up to you to always live purposefully on Cloud 9, viewing the world as amazing and colorful as it is.

For example, pay close attention to all the things you consider beautiful. I consider the sky beautiful. I love the clouds. I love the shapes they make. I love to make pictures of them. I love to just stare and marvel at God's amazing architectural designs. I give direct focus to everything. I focus on everything, and call it all great. Whatever you magnify, you will increase. That's just the law. Wherever you deposit your energy, whether negative or positive, you fertilize it with your actions.

If you are unable to achieve this sense of elation alone, then purchase motivational CDs, books, sermons, or whatever else is positive for you, and allow them to be your fuel. Read this book again and again every time you feel that you are falling into an emotional slump. Always know that I am here, rooting for you, praying for you, and cheering for your success. I may or may not know you personally, but what I do know is that we exist on the planet together as you are reading this book.

I didn't have to write the book, and you didn't have to read it. But we are here together, and I am very happy that you are reading right now, so I tell you again to be encouraged. You are on purpose. You are developing your gifts so you can begin to live your dream. You have overcome all those things from your past that were designed to destroy you. You are free. Your internal slave is free indeed. So be very careful that you are not enslaved again.

You have to purposefully decide to make changes that are beneficial to your life. It is a constant effort, but well worth it. Everything that is supposed to be in your life will begin to come in. There will be some people and some things that will be removed, and that may hurt. But you will be able to find joy because you will know that the outcome is beneficial for you. Remember, you are on purpose. Whatever your heart desires, you are supposed to have it. You must believe with your whole heart that you can have your desires. You must constantly encourage others, because when you do, you are encouraging yourself as well. You are allowing positive circumstances to enter into your life when you affect others positively. Everything you do for them, and to them, comes back to you in one way or another. This is also true when we affect people negatively. The negative things that you do and say come back to haunt you.

Within this book, I have repeated several phrases and will continue to do so because repetition is key to information retention. Why do you think that the Holy Bible is so repetitive? Please understand how important certain things are, such as reaping what you sow Clearly, when you plant a watermelon seed, you do not expect the watermelon to be the size of the seed. The watermelon will be extraordinarily bigger than the seed. In the same way, whatever you do comes back to you, only bigger—more or worse.

Therefore, motivation is crucial to our daily lives, even in our places of employment. If your boss has a negative attitude, and always has something condescending to say, how excited would you be to go to work? Probably not much at all. Everyone wants to be successful, but you first have to create a successful environment. Even if your boss is not so great, the way you handle him or her is crucial in whether you bring positive or negative energy into your life.

When you are excited about your work, you do things almost effortlessly, without being micromanaged. But the opposite is true when your attitude is negative. How much motivation do you really have? Being motivated to meet your goals is essential and can determine the quality of the outcome. Picture two equally qualified teams playing basketball. One team is excited and motivated. The other team is distracted. Which team do you think will win? Clearly, the team with the excitement and the motivation.

In a sports arena, fans can motivate their team. That's why most teams win on their home field or court more often than not. Motivation makes whatever you do exciting. It can even cause you to do more than you are required to do because of your heightened sense of excitement.

Let's continue walking into your purpose.

Chapter 6:

Want a Blessing? …Be One!

Most often it is the desire of everyone to be successful, to have great wealth, to drive a nice car, to live in a nice house, to have a nice family, to have a happy relationship that leads to a successful marriage, and to have productive functional children. These are the general desires of 99 percent of the world's population.

Even when those goals are achieved, it's usually a temporary opportunity because it isn't appreciated. Some people are just downright ungrateful. And the inability to show gratitude for anything that is presented to you or given to you is surely the easiest way to lose it quickly. Sometimes it's just the lack of understanding that causes the entire experience to be forfeited. You must be very careful to take purposeful consideration for everything and everyone in your life. You have to intentionally show your gratitude and your appreciation. Otherwise, you run the risk of losing it.

Showing gratitude is giving no focus whatsoever to things that are negative. It is clearly and intentionally paying direct attention to all that is positive. Sometimes it's not the easiest thing to do, but it is definitely the thing that will change your life. The more grateful you are for the things in your life, the more fulfilling your life will become. And as you begin to grow and understand your own life, gratitude will give you the ability to help others in their lives as well.

If there is something that you desire, believe it or not, you must give in order to receive. But keep in mind that you do not give with an expectation to receive. It is the law of life that you *will* receive because of your giving. Give and you shall be given even more. "For God so loved the world that he gave his only begotten son" (John 3:16). That is the key lesson on being a blessing. Whatever you love, you give. Giving is just like planting. If you plant a seed, surely the garden will grow. However, when you add fertilizer and other gardening products, you will reap a more productive harvest. It's the same in life.

Most often we put our money into the things we love. For example, take your bank statement and see what you spent the largest sums of money on. That is evidence of where your love is, regardless of whether you are able to admit this fact are not.

You can give without loving, but you cannot love without giving. God so *loved* the world that "HE GAVE." That is proof right there that love gives. He gave his only son because he loved. When you love, you give. God created loving and giving exactly this way so that we can see that it is in the sacrifice that we receive. And when you give, the law of life says that you will receive. That's just the cycle of giving.

Giving doesn't always mean things that are tangible or monetary. Giving has various meanings. It's whatever you release from yourself, whether it's your time, patience, understanding, or experience. You have treasures within you, including your passions, that can be shared with so many others, adding to the quality of their life. Quite naturally, we cannot leave out the giving of money. It is in giving monetary gifts that it is easiest to see where help is going.

Find yourself something to spend your money on that is beneficial to someone other than just yourself or your relatives.

Another great opportunity to give is to find charitable organizations that are benefiting great causes and building communities. There are all sorts of charitable organizations that add to the quality of life and well-being of people who are less fortunate than you. What you must understand is that there is always going to be someone who does not have as much as you have, or know as much as you know. Anything that you have much of requires much of you. Much requires much, and more requires more.

So be ready for the different levels of your life, and at every level increase the number of people that you help. No one can save the world, but it definitely does not hurt to try. Yes, money is very helpful and is required for us to have life's basic necessities, as well as a few extravagances. However, money is merely a tool. So be very careful not to let money become your God, causing you to lose focus of your destiny and your purpose in life. When you keep money in its perspective, you will bring more money into your life, and there's nothing wrong with having more of anything, including money.

What you have to realize is whatever it is that you want more of. You must give more of it as well. This does not mean that if you want $500, you have to give away $500. What it means is that you should continue giving to add increase. If you want love, you give love, and it will increase love in your life. If you want joy, make it a habit to intentionally bring joy to someone else's day, *every* day. If you desire others to be patient with you, you must be more patient yourself.

There is purpose, passion, and power inside you. You have just got to harness these things within yourself, and they will enable you to become a better you and give you the ability to become a huge blessing. There are so many people who are waiting for you and what you're going to contribute to the world. Do not let whatever situation you are in right now prevent you from achieving whatever it is you desire to achieve, as if you cannot move forward.

The passion that is inside you will pull you forward directly to your purpose. After reading this book, you will have the power to sustain yourself if you do not let externals influence you. This does not mean that life will come without opposition, but rather that you will recognize opposition before it can debilitate you.

There is always someone somewhere who needs exactly what you have to give. Don't let anyone convince you otherwise. If it is your desire to be a motivational speaker, and you know only ten people, start with them. If motivational speaking is your genuine desire, then it will come from a place of love and passion as you move naturally into whatever it is that you do.

Everyone wants a blessing, but being a blessing is the most wonderful thing you can be to anyone. Life gives us extensive opportunities to be a blessing to others, not only in things that are perceived as great, but in the simple things. It is the small things that we do for others that impact their lives forever. Although those things may seem simple to us, the effect that they have on the recipients can leave such an impact that those recipients in turn begin to help others.

Encouraging others at some of the lowest times in their lives is a great blessing. It is in those times of hopelessness and helplessness that people are the most debilitated. You have probably been there yourself. I know I have. It was in those times that the people who helped me so inspired me and elevated me financially, emotionally, and spiritually that now, when I reflect on them, even though I may have forgotten their names, I can pay it forward by helping others the way they helped me.

When people are hopeless and feel that they cannot go on, you can be a blessing to them if you provide a sense of sanity. The simple push that you gave them is what they needed, and often it's just a reminder of what is already inside them.

Being a blessing is giving without expectation. But giving to add to the quality of someone else's life or experience is also a blessing. Sometimes just an arrangement of words gives someone's life a fresh new meaning. In order to make this process completely effective, selfishness has to be banished. Selfishness is one of the most unhealthy characteristics that anyone can have. People are often unaware of their selfishness. If you are not sure whether or not you are selfish, then ask yourself this question: Are you always expecting and never giving? If so, that is a clear sign of selfishness.

Fortunately, one can become unselfish by instantly becoming a giver. If you are selfish with your time, give more time. If you are selfish with your money, give more of your money. If you are selfish with your love, be more loving. You can only benefit from giving because whatever you give, you get. So start being a blessing *right now*.

Find ways that you can give in all of the areas mentioned above. Make it a conscious effort to become a giver, starting *today*. Giving is crucial if you want to have a productive life. When you give, you release healthy endorphins that stimulate your brain. Not only is giving beneficial to the receiver, it is beneficial to the giver as well. Call someone you haven't spoken to in ages. Give time to family members that you rarely see. Give a little extra in your church offering. Give a little encouragement to a hurting friend.

When we all begin this conscious cycle of giving, we give to the universe, and in turn the universe gives back to us our hearts' desires. "Give, and it will be given to you. A good measure, pressed down, shaken together and running over, will be poured into your lap" (Luke 6:38).

Chapter 7:

Discovering Your

Purpose

Your purpose is already in you. If you feel as if you are not doing exactly what you were created do, that is only because you have not recognized your purpose yet. Most people are guilty of living a life that someone else thought for them. For example, parents often raise their children to do the things that they wish they had done. If a father wanted to be a football player and never got the opportunity to do so, it is almost a natural reaction for him to encourage his sons to play football.

Children adapt very well and generally take a liking to whatever it is that they're exposed to early in their lives, especially if they are encouraged by their parents. Most often, children like what they are exposed to. This does not necessarily mean that it is the purpose of any particular child to become a football player. The father has taken his own desire to be a ballplayer and attempted to live that wish vicariously through his child. But what happens when the child gets older and realizes that this dream was his dad's, not his own? Then the child probably changes his mind, and that can cause a rift in the parent-child relationship.

Or take cheer moms as an example. These are usually women who wish they had been cheerleaders themselves. Or else they enjoyed cheering so much that they assumed their daughters would, too. Exposed early enough to cheering, the young girl may in fact like it, due to her mom's excitement. This is most often the reason children follow the career paths of their parents. That is why exposure is extremely important.

The environment that we expose our children to will influence them positively or negatively, so we must be careful about what we expose them to. Due to positive exposure, we have generations of musicians, doctors, attorneys, and every other kind of worker. But some children have never been given the opportunity to explore and find their own passion and purpose. Parents, I urge you to give your children the opportunity to be themselves. You may not always agree with the things they do or the life choices they make, but no one can ever be completely happy by living someone else's dream.

Expose your children at a very early age to more than just the things that excite you. That broadens their horizons and gives them opportunities to find where their true passions lie. When they are exposed to more, and are given the chance to find out what it is they really love, there is a beautiful sense of peace that they recognize— and so do you!

I urge you to be open-minded with your children. In that way, you will create purposeful, functional adults who are being prepared early on to take the world by storm. Giving this opportunity to your children will prepare them for a more fulfilled life. Even though it may be very different from your own, it will begin to lead them to their own purpose.

You are the primary road map for your children. Although you do not know all the directions, you can show them the roads you have traveled and what you have learned on the way. To think like a child is the purest of actions. It is in these pure thoughts that true living lives. As a child, life is just a breeze. Your only requirement is to wake up, play, expect the best, and repeat the process. Life as an adult is just as beautiful, so wake up. Expect a great and wonderful day, and you will have one.

When you were a child, your imagination was huge. You believed that the possibilities were limitless. You believed in the Easter Bunny and Santa Claus and magic. You had no idea what had to happen. You just knew you would receive. Whatever it is that we received, it just showed up. Keep that same imagination, which is also known as faith. Faith is believing things that are yet unseen. One could say that faith is the relative of imagination.

As children, we simply know that our parents, caregivers, or other adults will provide most of the things that we need, but it is not our worry *how* to receive them. I am aware that many children do not receive exactly what they have wanted or needed, but the point I'm making here is that they must believe in order to receive.

That is the exact same thing that needs to happen to you as an adult. You must believe with childlike faith. To truly believe is to have limitless imagination, and know that all things are possible. Again, that is called faith. Having this belief and strong sense of

71

understanding ignites your sense of purpose even more. In your quest for recognizing your true purpose, look to the things that genuinely make you happy and excited. Those are the things that you can do effortlessly.

That is the driving force behind your passion; it is clearly your purpose. Your purpose brings you joy, happiness, and peace. It is the very thing that you will do even if you are not paid to do it. Becoming a millionaire is not a purpose; it is an accomplishment. Not everyone will become a millionaire, but everyone does have purpose, and when you begin to function properly in your purpose, becoming a millionaire will neither be important or unimportant. If it happens, of course you will be grateful. If it doesn't happen, you will not be debilitated, because when you're operating in your purpose, your millionaire resides in your spirit.

This is when your sense of self is priceless. Everything that you need and desire will be added to you because you are operating in your purpose. When you discover exactly what you are supposed to do in your life, that increases your excitement about life. We are all created uniquely and differently. Just like fingerprints, no two of us are alike. When you relax and stop trying to achieve the things that everyone else has, and truly identify with your inner self, ask yourself exactly what it is you have a passion to do. If you desire to be a millionaire, then take the necessary steps to become one, but that is not the desire of every single person in the world.

It is not your job to ridicule anyone else's life choices. When you give focus to what everyone else is doing, you don't have time to do what you were created to do. It takes every one of us to make this world go round, and the desires of every one of us are different—although sometimes they fall in the same category with those of millions of others.

There are millions of authors, but no two books are exactly the same. Books, like clothes, can sometimes be tailor-made, and I believe that this book was tailor-made just for you. What you receive from reading this book may be totally the opposite of what someone else receives from it. We all interpret information differently. But it is still the same book regardless of how it is received by each reader. The person you buy this book for will receive something totally different from what you intended. But neither of your opinions is wrong. It's just like a movie. Two people can watch the same movie and come away with different interpretations of it.

When you read a book, you begin to visualize and create your very own images in your mind of exactly how each character looks, down to the smallest detail. Then, to add to your great excitement, you hear that the book you read is going to be developed into a major motion picture. How exciting! This is one of your favorite books, and it's about to be turned into a movie. But when the movie is released, and you attend with your childhood excitement, you may be disappointed that more than half of the details are not what you imagined. You may walk away saying that the movie is nothing like the book, when it actually is. It's just that the director's vision is different from yours. That's what sets great directors apart—the ability to bring to life the majority of the vision so that the masses of America are attracted to the film, not just a select few.

Most of the directors who are considered great are following their purpose—the thing they do effortlessly. That does not mean that the process will be without struggle or work. What you thirst for drives you and gives you the most excitement. Yes, you will have to apply time and effort to your purpose, but you don't mind doing whatever it takes. So it is very important to begin to connect with people who are doing what you are doing, and learn and grow from them.

I remember that, even when I was a little girl, I wanted to have a daughter. I thought, when I grow up I'm going to have a little girl, and she's going to be just like me. I had her name all picked out ever since I was in high school. I was going to name her Savannah Reign. It would have been spelled exactly like that because a savannah is a large grassland in a tropical region, and to me her first name would have meant that the possibilities for her would be endless. Tropical brings to my mind images of beautiful flowers and joyful experiences. Reign would be spelled exactly like that because I knew that she would have the ability to rule, the strength to encourage, and the power to be exactly who she was. Savannah *would* Reign.

That sounds lovely, doesn't it? But, as it turned out, I do not have a biological daughter—although I did have the opportunity to assist in raising my stepdaughter and my little cousin. I never gave birth to a daughter of my own, but Savannah's name never left me, and as time progressed after my divorce, I founded a nonprofit organization, which I named it GyyC, standing for Gyrl. Yes, You Can! I selected that name because I believe that anyone just has to be willing to try, and sometimes you need the necessary push to make you to want to try. I am also living proof that gyrl, yes, you can. I believe it is my purpose to pour into these young ladies everything that I myself did not get.

We cannot repeat our lives, but what we can do is see someone going through unnecessary phases and stages that we've already traveled, and we can lighten their loads some. We cannot make a mistake for them, but we can definitely warn them so that they don't have to stay in situations any longer than necessary to receive their conditioning for living. Or should I say their preparation for their purposes? I teach them to understand the dysfunctions of life. I share with them my life and the horrible choices I made.

How does all this tie in together? I'm glad you're wondering. God did not give me a daughter. However, he gave me many daughters. At the end of the program, the girls receive the Savannah Reign Award. So every girl leaves with a little bit of Savannah Reign. I love them so much, and I know they love me.

My organization has only been around for two years, and I was hesitant to start it for lack of funding, lack of knowledge, and lack of everything. But I went forward. I had a close friend who allowed me to come into her middle school after-school program. I used all of my own resources for purchasing the things for them. Periodically, I would have friends donate money as well as items to the girls, but for the most part I carried the weight and didn't mind doing so at all.

God put in my spirit that every time I speak to them I must bring gifts. I didn't understand that at first, especially since I myself was struggling, but it was a discipline for me, and I followed through and continue to follow through.

The minimum number of gifts that I bring is three. What I bring always changes. I use the number three because it is my favorite. It is significant to me for many reasons. The primary reason is the Holy Trinity, but I'll talk about that later. You see, it was within my lack that my greatest gift resided. All of my pain, all of my early childhood traumas, all the things that I did not get have given me the ability to give so freely and to find my purpose. Some people may have just one thing in life that they desire to do. Some may wish to be teachers, and they might teach for fifty years before retiring and living happily ever after. There are other people, such as me, who have many desires within them. Don't let anyone tell you that you're doing too much. The problem is you're doing more than they are. God does not put more on you than you can bear, whether troubles or blessings. Whatever your purpose is, and whatever the desires are in your heart, provisions will be made to achieve them.

When I operated an organization purely out of the kindness of my heart, God saw fit for someone to offer me the opportunity to be the events coordinator of a bigger girls' group, which meets three times a year. How blessed am I for this new opportunity! It will surprise you in ways beyond your own imagination how surrendering yourself to others will open up your purpose to you.

Your purpose will make your enemies bless you. Don't let lack stop you. Lack shows you that it was God, not you, who increased your blessing. Yes, it is great to have the perfect business plan all lined up exactly the way it should be. There are people for whom that is the way things happen. If you are one of them, I applaud you. Having a plan and a strategy is definitely a clear focused way to go, but sometimes life doesn't happen like that.

It certainly did not in my own case. I work daily to perfect the areas where I am still incomplete, but I cannot wait until I believe that I am the perfect person to do what is in me. No one is perfect, and no one ever will be. So if you're waiting for perfection, you'll be waiting a long time.

You may have something that you have always longed to do.

Then, that could be your purpose. If you are not operating in your purpose, you are merely existing, whether or not you are comfortable. If you do not have passion for what you do in life, you will be left with a feeling of emptiness. If you feel that you do not fit into your job environment and that you're forcing situations, then that job is probably not your purpose.

Many people live their entire life never finding their true purpose. I heard of a man in New York who was on Wall Street, making millions, but he was not happy. He quit his job and opened a hot dog stand. To his surprise and delight, the hot dog stand became a major success. Part of the reason was that he had the necessary capital. But the moral of the story is that he found internal happiness, and that brought him financial success.

There are people all over the world who finally find themselves and give up everything to live their true passion. At last, they relinquish the dreams of everyone around them. The childhood football team or cheerleading squad no longer exists for them, and they become a person of their own. For example, consider Jennifer Hudson's husband. He was an attorney, but he desired to be a wrestler, and now he is one. Until you live your life doing exactly

79

what you want, you will never truly live.

Your purpose could easily be the very thing that upsets you the most. For example, if there is something that constantly nags at you, and you see how it could be different, it could very well be your assignment to change it or to make it better. If you are an advocate against domestic violence, it could be your purpose to open a shelter for abused women. And in the process, that might well become your source of income, and you may also be able to provide jobs for others. If something upsets you, the natural reaction is to try to change it. And finding your purpose in that process is always rewarding. You are giving, and you will receive.

Your purpose is in you, whether you recognize it or not. It will be there throughout your continuous mistakes until you have abandoned it long enough to recognize it or take it to the grave with you, having never lived on purpose. What a sad thought! But you don't have to do that if you decide to live your purpose now.

Reflect back on your childhood and the pain you experienced back then. Most of the time, your purpose comes from your pain. Your purpose is clearly yours. It is not the dream of others trying to do what is designed for someone else to do. Another person cannot be your purpose and can never fulfill you completely. People come and go, but your purpose is in you forever. Your purpose is something that you are extremely passionate about. The passion that you have for whatever it is you desire to do is proof that the desire is your purpose.

Most importantly, you have to associate with people who believe in your dreams much as you do, and support you. My business partner, who is also my cousin and best friend, as well as my closest confidant, not only sees the vision for the business adventures we have, such as GyyC, but she takes the vision and makes it her own. I see and feel her passion as though it were mine.

God will assemble a team who will assist you in fulfilling your dream. At the same time, you must be eager to help others on their purpose trail. The most successful people in life push others to succeed. You cannot achieve success alone. It takes others to assist you. How you treat them will determine how long they'll be there for you. Treat them with dignity and respect, and you will have them at your side for a lifetime. But being ungrateful will drive them away as fast as they came.

Even in preparing this book, I had help. This is my first book, and all I had at first was a dream. But there were people who saw the dream and got behind it and helped to make it happen. I even utilized the funding program called Kickstarter. There were people whose names you will read at the back of the book who believed enough in this book's purpose to help in the editing process by pledging their assistance, and I thank each and every one of you from the bottom of my heart every day. This book would not be in your hands now if it weren't for the Kickstarters who backed it.

Finding your actual purpose in life is surrendering yourself and following your passion. The purpose of living is a state of mind. It is a choice to always see the glass a completely full, and to always expect the best and know that, in the end, you will win. Every day you wake up, the first words out of your mouth should be, "Thank you!" The ability to speak is enough to be grateful for. Always know that someone somewhere is in a worse situation than you are. Your state of mind is the most important part of your purpose. When the enemy can control your mind, he controls your entire life. Every day, you must be intentionally happy, intentionally positive, and intentionally in motion. Then the universe will allow everything intentional to come your way.

Chapter 8:
Getting Rid of
Procrastination

Procrastination is the number one killer of success. Do you sit around talking about what you're going to do, but never get anything done? Or do you simply do just enough to get by on a daily basis? There are so many dreams and goals that live inside you that have not had the opportunity to be born. But you only do what you need to do to achieve the bare minimum. This means waking up each day, only doing the necessary things, such as getting dressed, going to work, taking care of children, bringing in an income, coming home, and repeating the same cycle again, but never feeling fulfilled.

You know that there is something else you should be doing. The hollowness inside you is evidence that you are not living your purpose. Living your purpose gives you an irreplaceable richness in your spirit. Most of the time, that alone brings you to a place of financial stability and sometimes great wealth. If that sounds familiar, then this chapter is for you.

This chapter was and is definitely for *me*. In writing this book, I had to reread it several times, and it is this chapter that made me want to mash the gas on my life and begin operating in my God-given purpose. I realized that I often spoke about goals, ideas, and dreams, but rarely took the necessary steps to complete those tasks. I had no idea why I behaved like that, because in my mind all of the ideas were perfect and would not only bring wealth to me, but also benefit others. I found myself desiring to do anything that would motivate other people, but usually doing very little or just enough to begin the necessary steps.

This is the chapter of all chapters. This is the chapter in which we *make it happen*. Believe it or not, this book almost did not get written, because of *procrastination*. Procrastination is a disease that keeps you stagnant and in bondage. You have to free yourself from it. It does not allow you to live the purposeful life you were born to live.

What happens is that you unconsciously block and condition your mind to believe "I will do it later." But it never gets done. Days, weeks, months, even years pass, when you could have accomplished so much more. Procrastination definitely blocks you from your purpose.

Today is the day that you will be delivered from procrastination. From this day forward, when the thought of *doing it later* comes to your mind you *must* immediately follow through and not wait. Not moving swiftly enough not only hinders you, but many others as well. Whether you know it or not, your purpose is attached to the lives of many others. Someone somewhere is waiting for exactly what you have to offer. So every time you feel the spirit of procrastination seeping in, come to Chapter 8. You can actually start right here over again. To help you find it, let's put a helpful reminder right here:

MY PURPOSED LIFE BEGINS HERE

Everything is on *purpose* when you are truly listening with your spirit to life and everything that's going on in it. Phenomenal unexplainable things happen often, so pay close attention, as will I, because there is a message here for everyone. Let's get to it. Let's assassinate the assassinator, known by the name of Sir Procrastination. I'm excited. I hope you are, too.

Believe it or not, your procrastination is not yours alone. There are all sorts of influences around, including people, that subliminally encourage you not to succeed. Don't get me wrong; it may not be intentional. I did say subliminal. But their behavior, their opinions of your goals, their lack of enthusiasm, and their unwillingness to see your vision may cause you to stumble, or to doubt yourself and your vision. Some of those people could be the closest ones to you, the ones you love most dearly. More than likely, these are the people whose opinions you have allowed to construct or destruct your own aspirations. What you have to remember is that living your purpose is never intended to hurt anyone. If anyone is ever hurt by you living your purpose and the will that God has for you, then they are being selfish and do not have your best interests in mind.

What you have to know is that living your life on purpose is not always going to be easy. You lose a lot of people that you thought would be there forever, and that is an extremely harmful process. But it must be done in order for you to achieve your true purpose and not become the passion of someone else's purpose.

There will be times that you will feel alone, but do not be alarmed. You will not be alone long on your path to success. You have to truly begin to align yourself mentally for this deliverance of procrastination and of people who affect you negatively and encourage your procrastination.

There are two entities in this world: good and evil. If you remove an *o* from *good*, you've got *God*. If you add a *D* in front of *evil*, you've got *Devil*. Let's associate positive and negative to good and evil, respectively—or to God and the Devil. If you have positive energy, you have good energy, or God energy. If you have negative energy, that is evil energy, or of the Devil.

Clearly, there is a hindrance in anything negative. It is crucial for you to pay attention to the actions and reactions of other people when you share your purpose and your vision. If they are not moving in the direction you want them to go, then it's probably time to start doing some serious evaluating and preparing yourself for things that may hurt you, but won't kill you. Don't let anyone hold your past against you. You are you, regardless of what you have done, how you have done it, or who you have done it to.

Let it all go! You do that by knowing that you're right where you're supposed to be right now. Regardless of your history, you are about to create your future. Be grateful for everything that you have experienced in the past. It was because of those things that you are who you are. God made you great. Therefore, you *are* great. Nothing and no one can take your greatness from you.

Consider a king who makes poor decisions, which causes him to lose most of his subjects, who change their allegiance to another kingdom. Now, instead of ruling over 100,000 people, he only rules over 10,000. Realize that his diminishment had a purpose, because his rule over his former kingdom is over, and now he's in a smaller arena. But God has forgiven the king because he meant well, and God knew his heart. The king, although reduced in power, is just as great as he was before. He's still a king, because the king-ness is inside him.

Naturally, when someone falls from position, there are consequences, but this did not change the king's greatness; it only reduced the number of people under his authority. When facing the consequences of poor choices, one must face the music and dance the best dance. Give your all wherever you are, despite what you're going through. None of that matters. Hold your head up despite your mistakes. Wherever you are in life is exactly where you should be. Your place in life has absolutely nothing to do with the life of anyone else. How far ahead of you they are should not matter. And you should definitely not look down on other people for what they have not accomplished, because that only brings negativity to you. To compare yourself to someone else leaves you in a place of internal confusion. You are exactly who you are, and it is important that you accept the you that you are right now. If there are some things about yourself that you desire to change, change them.

Feelings of unworthiness and fear are another reason why people procrastinate. If you allow fear to be the driving force of your life, your life will be motionless. Fear is a lack of faith. Most of the time, fear comes from being afraid to fail. If you have not heard that before, let me be the first one to tell you that behind every success is a failure. Besides, without failing you have nothing to measure succeeding by. Let nothing in your life make you feel unworthy. Everyone makes mistakes. As long as we live, we will make them.

Mistakes are just that: mis-takes. It's how you handle them that determines the outcome of all situations, so do not let a setback in life cause you to surrender your purpose. It may cause temporary halts, but never let it stop you.

You're not the first person to go through what you're experiencing, and you certainly won't be the last. Society may say one thing, but you can't live your life based on the opinions of others. People will tell you their preferences and opinions all the time. The good news is, that doesn't matter, one way or the other. Criticism is wonderful when it's constructive, but guard yourself against negative criticism.

God has placed destiny in you and the desires that are in you. If you live by society's terms or to please people, you will forever be chasing your tail. But if you pay attention to the desires in your own heart and rid yourself of motionless living, procrastination will become a thing of the past, because you will be paying attention to your purpose in seeking divine direction. When procrastination or any other negative energy is in your presence, use your intuition to recognize this disguise. Quickly realize that it's the trick of the enemy, grab your bags, and keep moving.

There's purpose in you, and there are things that you need to do. There are people that you need to see and places that you need to be. Don't be alarmed. Be prepared. You are destined and purposed for greatness. Not everyone is a reader, and not everyone reads an entire book, but you've come this far. The good news is that procrastination did not stop you from reading, so don't let it stop you in your purpose.

Let's just say that you don't finish reading this book, but just stop somewhere in this chapter. As I wrote this book, prayer was my primary focus, even for people who do not finish it. I believe that this book will have so much power that by merely touching it, you will begin to heal in the areas you need to. The words somehow seep into crevices of your mind, your heart, and your soul, and give you the extra push out of procrastination into your destination.

It's time that you totally understand that your life is not your own, that it is a gift. And while this gift is still in your hands, you have the opportunity to make it the best yet.

You have to know that you were born with a purpose. You must also know that there is a great work that can be done through you. You are as great as you believe you are. Death and life are in the power of the tongue. Whatever you curse in your life will be cursed. Whatever you speak life into and bless will have life.

As this book travels across the world, I pray that it will pick up an unexplainable momentum. If the book has provided any insights to you and opened your eyes at all, please tell people about it, even if you have to give away your own copy—especially if you see someone hurting, and you think the book can open up their hearts and minds to help them through their circumstances. There's always healing as we help one another.

There is never a reason to quit. Look up because everything you need is above you. Have you ever noticed that the negative sign is in a horizontal position and keeps you flat lined. But the positive sign has a vertical line that is rising. Everyone wants to elevate to higher levels in life. The vertical line coupled with a horizontal line is proof that life will not be completely without negativity. But you do not have to give focus to what is negative.

As soon as you change your mind, there will be doors of opportunity opening up instantly, because you opened up the gratitude airways for positivity to find you. At the same time, you also find your purpose. There is greatness on the other side of procrastination, so you better get there. Procrastination doesn't wait. It weighs you down. Whenever you decide to rid yourself of procrastination, but you feel it slipping back in, immediately take a quick dose of medicine called "Get up and do it anyway." That method has a 100 percent success rate. Do a little bit more today than you did yesterday. That will get you closer to your desires every day.

If your desire is to become a master chef, you can do that. But you can't do it if no one tastes your cooking. You must take the necessary steps to get yourself in the arenas to be exposed, and your food tasted. Realistically speaking, if no one ever tastes your cooking, what are the chances of becoming a master chef? Have you heard of opportunists? That word is usually considered bad. However, opportunists are seeking opportunities, and reaching aggressively toward their goals. So long as do it with pure intentions, they will get my attention over procrastinators any day.

There are people in foreign countries who will do anything to come to America. There are so many opportunities here that are missed because of procrastination. Some foreign countries offer very few if any opportunities, which is why many impoverished people from those countries dream of coming to America. When they do finally get the opportunity to come here, they are usually more successful than Americans because of their intense focus. Things that we take for granted, such as TVs, cell phones, or computers, are major luxuries to them. Therefore, they do not have a preconceived selfish greed. They are most often seeking a better life, one only dreamed of and found in America. Once they succeed, their sense of gratitude usually leads them, not to seek materialistic things, but to help their families and villages back home.

In America, because of the freedoms here, opportunities are taken for granted. What you must recognize is that opportunity gives you chances. You must realize that opportunities surround you. You must accept that opportunities require work. The most important thing about opportunities is that if you do not recognize them, the window will close.

Chapter 9:

Don't Dish It..., If You

Can't Take It

I don't mean to come out of the cage swinging, but there are some very necessary truths that I need to share with you. Many of you who are reading this book right now either grew up in a blended family, or have one now. If this topic has completely missed you, then I'm sure you at least know someone from a blended family who could use the information I am about to give. Do share it with them.

A blended family is one that is formed and made up of children from previous marriages or relationships. As increasingly common as this type of family is, it is not without its share of dysfunctions. Please understand that the way you treat your stepchildren is crucial.

The way you interact with them is not only conducive to their well-being, but to the success of the marriage as well. Being negative or counterproductive to children will not only cause problems in your marriage, but the energy that you've created will return to you outside the home as well. You cannot mistreat anyone intentionally or unintentionally and expect life not to give you a dose of your own medicine.

When family issues consist of my child versus your child, as well as tit-for-tat situations, things only get worse. This is one of the primary reasons for dysfunctions in families, and also creates dysfunctional children. This can be prevented by intentionally focusing on the positive things your spouse's children do, instead of the negative things. Make sure that you give the children the necessary tools for living, such as love, guidance, discipline, instruction, and responsibility, regardless of whether the children are biologically yours or not.

Some parents in blended families have more tolerance for their biological children than for their nonbiological children. Their biological children tend to get away with more behavior that deserves discipline. Nonbiological parents sometimes feel inadequate when it comes to disciplining the children of their spouse. Not to discipline children shows a lack of love, which is a form of neglect. Love disciplines. God's word is that to spare the rod is to spoil the child. But the punishment does not always have to be corporal. It can be a stern talking to. Both parents need to comfort, love, give to, share with, care for, discipline, and guide their children, biological or not.

I know these things are easier said than done, but they can all be accomplished. Remember that kids are people too, and they also have to deal with this blended family that you have put them into. The easiest way to handle this type of situation is to look at a child and mentally remove his or her face, replacing it with your own. Look into the child's eyes not as if they were your own, and you can see from the child's perspective. There in front of you is little *you* needing *you*. How would you treat you? How would you nurture you? What would you say to you that you need to hear? What would you give to you that you didn't get? How would you embrace you? What would you do to ensure that you have the life you want to live?

Pick yourself up and give yourself a hug and a kiss, and tell yourself that everything is going to be okay. I know that I'm not your father or mother, but I will do everything I can to help you to become the best you that you can be. Wouldn't you want adults to give you that kind of love? Wouldn't it be amazing to be told how wonderful you are? I know you would love it, because I'm loving writing about it. As the child receives your words, I can visualize and see his or her shoulder blades spreading wide like wings.

The children you are raising now, whether they are 7 or 17, need all of that. And your reward will be great, because you are being faithful to those precious gifts that God has given you. You are still a stepparent and a very necessary part of the nurturing of your nonbiological children. Believe it or not, it helps your marriage, too. If you pay no attention to anything else in this book, please begin to nurture and mold the wonderful blessings that God has given you, regardless of how he gave them to you. Children are a blessing at any age, and none of them asked to be here.

Children have to learn to play cards with the hand they have been dealt, but you're the dealer, so why not intentionally give them a full house? You are the nurturer, biological or not. God trusted you. Put every effort into providing the skills for living and love that each child needs. You will see that it will not only benefit the child, but your entire household, and your life outside the home as well. The benefit of this is that the child, and life itself, will reward you even more. Remember, whatever you do is going to be returned to you. This is your opportunity to make sure your return is fantastic.

This is a perfect opportunity to speak a little bit more about what not to dish if you can't take it. Some lessons in life are hard-learned lessons. As I stated in the Preface, I was married at one time. That gave me the opportunity to look back and evaluate marriage as a whole. What I have concluded is that a wife must be her husband's mistress, business partner, and wife—in that order—all the time.

The mistress is not concerned about the wife. Her ultimate intent is to purposely distract her man and try to do everything better. She is not concerned with the bills, his family, or even her own. She just wants to ensure that he has a good time. She takes the necessary steps to look amazing. Whenever she sees him, she expects intimacy, and gives it to him as if it's their first time, *every* time.

The business partner could not care less about his private life, his wife, or his mistress. She wants to make sure that all of the business ventures add up, all of the deals are closed, and all of the *i*'s are dotted and the *t*'s crossed.

The wife is the most important role of all, because she is where the heart and home are. She is the man's balance. She is his nurturer. She prides herself on taking care of her family by paying the bills, running the household, and making sure the children are where they're supposed to be. She is connected to his family.

The beautiful part is, all of these roles are you: *the Wife*. You are all three roles, but you must be careful not to mix them. Using this system will definitely create a wonderful peace in your home and excitement in your love life. Keep in mind that at the end of the day, when you guys have settled down, and your husband is looking for intimacy, do not bring the problems of the day into the bedroom. That does not mean that the problems do not exist—just that this is not the time to discuss them.

You have to intentionally change your mindset in order to separate yourself into these three roles. Having these separate connections will create a marital bliss that neither one of you will be able to explain. It will just be good, *real* good. Do not allow the daily activities of being a wife to cause you to forget the duties of being the mistress. Remember that it is important to be a mistress first, so that you make your husband remember why he married you in the first place. When it's time to be the mistress, totally get into character and forget about the wife and the family's problems. That will make for a happy husband and marriage.

When it's time to be a wife, take care of the duties at home. You are capable and strong, so you can handle it all. You signed up for the role of wife. You said, "I do." So accept your position with pride, honor, and grace. You are the nurturer, so not only do your children look up to you, but your husband looks *to* you. When he's asking you questions, and you get that feeling that he's making you into his mother, do not perceive it that way. Be grateful that he loves you so much that he can put his guard down and be vulnerable with you. A man does not show everyone his sensitive side. But every man has one. After all, we were created from the rib of man. And he will return to us for that sensitive connection. So, do not confuse that with dependency on you. Instead, view it as trust in you. He is still every bit a man.

Being the business partner is quite simple; just handle your business. Allow your man to be the leader of your home, regardless of whether or not you agree with every decision he makes. The ability to have a discussion and agree is awesome. But when a family decision needs to be made, whether you agree with him or not, let your man be a man—even if you just have to help him find his socks.

Do not think for a minute, husbands, that you are off the hook. No, sirs! You have three roles as well. You must remember that you are her boyfriend, who tells her that she's the most beautiful girl in the world. She needs to know how amazing she is. She needs to hear you say how sexy she is. She needs that unexpected pinch here and there. She needs that gentle whisper in her ear. Sexy texts throughout the day make for wonderful evenings. She doesn't want to hear complaints about what she did or didn't do. When she's with her boyfriend, she doesn't want to talk about her husband. She wants her boyfriend to make her feel like a schoolgirl again. Reassure her that she is your primary focus and number one priority. Most importantly, let her know that there's no place else on Earth that you would rather be than in her arms.

As the business partner, you keep the family's best interests at hand, so that you don't send your family to the poorhouse. And know that there are children who need a father's love. Knowing that daddy loves them just as much as mommy does makes for an amazing home. I am so excited for you guys at the thought of how happy your marriages will be. Marriage is a wonderful God-given gift, to be respected and appreciated. Your woman needs to know that she could fall back into your arms blindfolded and trust that you will be there to catch her. Couples need to know that whether or not they are multimillionaires or life takes a turn for the worst, they have each other.

If you are not married, consider all of these things before tying the knot. Remember, not everyone is designed for marriage, because whatever you bring to any relationship, you will get more of it back, whether negative or positive. Marriage is a unity that is to be respected.

Just as a farmer does not walk into a field and wish for his crop, he must take the necessary steps to bring it forth. It is not enough just to toss seeds onto the ground. You must provide proper nutrients, or there will be no harvest. That is why the early stages of gardening are so important. First of all, you must make sure that you have taken the necessary preparatory steps. If you intend to grow something, you must first make sure that the plants you want are in season. If you plant out of season, very little, if anything, will bloom.

This is true of life in general. When it is time to accomplish some purpose, you must do what is necessary for you to put yourself in the right position and season. Connect with the right people, and have the attitude necessary to make that happen. This means being extremely careful about how you treat others. Like everything else, after you have planted the seed, it begins to take root. So if you plant seeds of malice, your evil intent, although covered up temporarily like a seed with dirt, will bloom and be visible to everyone. We are all guilty of having planted things that we were not happy about. If you believe this is not true of you, then I believe you're being dishonest with yourself.

For those of you who know that there was a point in time in your lives that you planted bad seeds, it is now time to dig up those roots. You must plant new seeds—seeds that you want to see harvested in your own life, the lives of people around you, and in everything you do.

Now that it's time to plant, pick a place in your life that you want to begin the healing process. Work the ground. Remove the bad dirt and replace it with good dirt. You have no reason to continue living a fictitious life. You don't have to live a life for others. You must live in peace and understanding of all that you are and all that you are becoming. Start by purifying your mind, your actions, and your thoughts. All of these things play into who you are and who you will become, and they are affected by the seeds you plant.

This does not mean that everything will be peaches and cream. Even after you have planted a flower, weeds will begin to grow around it. If you remove the weeds, you may kill the flower or damage the root. Recognize that the flower is still a flower in the midst of the weeds. The flower has not changed its identity, although it is surrounded by unnecessary issues in life—or what you think is unnecessary because you are unable to recognize that everything that happens is on purpose. After the flower blooms and you pluck it to be part of a bouquet, it has served its purpose. Furthermore, the weeds can be removed, so they do not return next season.

It is necessary to get rid of the things that are not beneficial in your life. Sometimes these may be people. This is your life, and in order to live it completely on purpose, you cannot be what someone else wants you to be for their sake. It hurts when you lose some things and some people. But that's okay. It is all for a good cause.

Remember that it's for you and your purpose on this planet, so clearing the ground makes way for you to make things better.

You begin by improving the soil. You bring in the things that are beneficial to you. Believe it or not, those things will find you because your spirit is calling them. We are spiritual beings. Your flesh would not have a voice if your voice did not have a soul. Your soul was somewhere before you were even formed in your mother's womb. You must nurture and help your soul to find its short existence here on Earth. Your soul is a gift to your flesh right now. The question is, what will you do with it while it's in you? Carefully choose the people and situations that you allow into your life, because they make impressions on your being. Whatever you do, and whoever you come into contact with, will have some kind of effect on you, whether positive or negative. So you have to make a conscious effort to nurture your goals, dreams, and ideas with water for life. For me that is the word of God.

Watering your life brings forth your purpose, so you must cover yourself with spiritual mulch—namely, mentors, spiritual leaders, and advisors. They will serve as a mulch for your life. Now you are on your way. Continue to take care of your garden and watch it grow. Continue to add the water and pay attention to the mulch. If you see weeds when they are small, pull them out. But if they insist on staying, make sure your flower is in full bloom, because the weeds will weed out themselves. As my bishop says, "You'll get that one on the way home."

Be careful what you wish for, because you just might get it. Just as God is our heavenly father, we are his children. When our children ask us for candy when we know that they haven't eaten nutritious food yet, sometimes we still give it to them, just because they ask. Sometimes God gives us things just because we ask. Even when those things are not necessary, he wants us to have the desires of our heart. So if your heart desires something that is not conducive to your goals, you will sometimes be awarded those things.

But it is a different story when you can deny your selfish desires and only want what is necessary, even if that causes you fleshly pain. That's okay. When you develop the ability to deny yourself, that's when you have really begun to live on purpose. That is a struggle for many people, including me. But I promise you I do not struggle with that issue with the same intensity that I used to, because I understand that living purposely on Cloud 9 requires a conscious effort.

Have I always been positive? Absolutely not! I was in pain because of my negativity. I had no idea why I was negative. I thought I was a bad person because I was negative, but that was not the case. I thought I had no reason to be positive. I took a mental walk down memory lane, and saw no joy in the life of that child. Everything that happened to her was unhappy, and I felt a sudden sense of empathy for her and realized then that the key to my purpose was in my past. It is now my destiny to purposefully be positive. I can no longer be negative.

Am I 100 percent positive all the time? Again, absolutely not. But when I feel negative energy, I immediately and consciously change it into positive energy, even in conversation. If a conversation begins to take a negative twist, I immediately look for something positive. That is what you must do because everything you say that is negative affects the person you're speaking to, and it affects you. What comes out of your mouth affects you.

Take reality TV, for example. People want to escape from their own realities. I'm guilty of watching a few of those shows, too, and sometimes find myself shaking my head in disbelief. But let me serve notice to you. All of these things that you are ingesting are getting into your spirit. Whether you want to believe that or not, it is true. We live in a real world. Some of it is interesting, funny, ridiculous, unbelievable, and superficial, and definitely draws us in. But be careful of the things that draw you in. If you are ingesting nothing but drama, you will bring that drama to you. Just like food, it may fill you up until you decide to push it away. If you don't, that may lead to gluttony. And the gluttony that it will lead to in this case will be unnecessary experiences in your own life. If you don't believe me, just keep watch those programs, and see what happens in your own life.

My prayer is that your consumption of this book will assist you to find the necessary balance in life. I want you to understand that it is possible to live up to the potential that is already inside you. But there will be things from which you will have to disconnect. As you grow, you will begin to know what things to move. And as you detach, you will realize that the things that used to attract you now disgust you. You can elevate yourself to heights that you never dreamed, not just in your own life, but in the lives of everyone you come into contact with.

Most of the time, reality TV has a negative impact on its viewers, because they are consuming all of the drama, chaos, and madness that is occurring within the show. You look at the characters and measure their lives against your own experiences. Usually, these shows are purposeless and meaningless. What they have done is found a way to capitalize on all of the dysfunctions of people who are willing to expose themselves to the world. Because those people are most often celebrities, the viewers want to know what's going on in their lives.

People mask their own pain by watching the pain of others. Everyone knows that reality TV sells controversy and sex. Sad but true. It is a known fact that Kim Kardashian has more followers on Twitter than the president of the United States of America. People are more concerned with nonsense than they are with the state of the country. Don't get me wrong. I'm not criticizing Kim Kardashian or the Kardashian brand. I personally think her mom is a marketing genius. Most often, viewers want to see the reality stars make fools of themselves or at least provides standards to measure their own dysfunctions by.

So when you purposely tune into these shows, please be aware that you are inviting negative energy into your life. When you tune into shows that are negative or positive, the energy goes both ways. They're both magnified when you invite them in. Which do you really want to be your guest? That is something you should think about and consider every single time you decide to watch anything on television.

I have noticed that many of the people who are on television do not realize their true potential. They have the opportunity to affect the masses because they have a large viewing audience, so it's always beautiful when these reality stars have a lightbulb moment, or what Oprah calls an aha moment, realizing that the opportunity they have been given is huge, since they can have a positive impact on thousands, if not millions, of lives. The thought of it brightens my heart.

As you read this book, I hope it opens your mind so much that your taste for negativity has been expunged. No one's purpose on this planet is to be an idiot, although some people have made millions doing so. Most of the time, such people do not have a happy life, since money does not buy inner peace. Just think of the life of the infamous Michael Jackson. He seemed to have everything in the world, but what he wanted most was that we take him for granted.

You must intentionally recognize the greatness within you, and not allow society to fill you up with negative issues. Notice that the shows that last the longest are the ones with the most drama, because they provide a subliminal pool to keep you in your own constant turmoil. The enemy loves company.

This is not to say that positive programs on television do not last. They do. But TV needs more positive people on it, who will influence others to live purposely on Cloud 9. Everyone should want to have a positive impact on the world. The easiest way to do that is to live your life purposefully.

Chapter 10:
The Lives of Others
Depend on You

The reason why you were born was to serve others, period. There are no *ifs*, *ands*, or *buts* about it. When you understand that life is not about you, but about what you do purely for others, that is when you will really have begun to live your life's purpose. You have been given gifts, but they are not yours alone. They must be shared. And your gifts will pay you.

For example, the editor of my book takes pride in his job, which pays him as well as giving him opportunities to exercise his talents. You cannot be selfish, because selfishness brings nothing to you but pain. Sure, there are people who appear to be selfish and blessed. But it is not your responsibility to concern yourself with the lives of others. They will be held accountable for their own actions. When you busy yourself with unnecessarily worrying about others and their situations, you become careless in your own affairs. In any case, Biblical Scripture states that the wealth of the wicked is stored up for the just. The only way to receive is to give. Whatever you are receiving the most of it is what you are knowingly or unknowingly giving the most of.

So if you want to truly live, you must begin to serve your purpose wholeheartedly. The way you do that is have a free, joyous attitude in all situations. Don't busy yourself with the simple worries of life. To worry is not to have faith, and you cannot do both. If you have made mistakes in your life, and others are holding you accountable, that is not your fault. Forgive yourself and allow life to give to you.

If you have a dream or a desired goal planted inside you, what would be the purpose of living the dream or fulfilling that goal if there were no one to share or enjoy it with you? It would be purposeless. Everything we do in life, we do for others.

I wrote this book because of all the painful things I have endured in my life. They left me clueless and lonely in a world that was so big that, at times, it seemed that I was becoming more and more invisible by the day. That's because I did not understand who I was, nor did I comprehend my life or my purpose.

I have lived in many places with many people. There are even people and situations in my life that I have totally forgotten. Because of my extremely unstable childhood, there are a vast number of people who know me more than I know them. Sometimes people tell me stories about myself that I clearly do not remember. Sometimes their stories remind me of what happened, but most often the memories are vague.

The fact that I do not completely remember some parts of my own life breaks my heart. I believe that there is an area of my mind that I have unconsciously blocked. One time, when I was at my youngest son's peewee football game, a lady walked up to me and asked me if I remembered her. I told her that she looked familiar, but that's as far as I could go. She told me that we were pregnant at the same time as teens, and that I had told her that her child would be ugly and have nappy hair like hers. When she told me that, it broke my heart.

I asked if I could speak with her alone. When we got away from people, I told her that I did not remember the incident at all, and asked why I had said such a thing. She said she had no idea. After I asked her a few more questions, I concluded that I had been jealous because she seemed so happy. Her mother brought her to school every day, whereas I didn't have a mother. Needless to say, I apologized for my rude teenage behavior, and she was very receptive. This story demonstrates how hurt people hurt people.

If you are reading this book, and I have affected you negatively in some way in the past, knowingly or unknowingly, please forgive me. I apologize with my whole heart. If you have read this far, I am certain that you are aware that that Brisha was then, and this one is now. I am so grateful that I have become the person I am today.

You cannot hold yourself accountable for what people remember about you. If someone reminds you of something negative you did to them, please seek forgiveness from them. At the same time, forgive yourself. You cannot make anyone else forgive you, for people process their own pain in their own time. You cannot live purposely if you are harboring ill feelings and unforgiveness, which must be released. Those things are all a part of your past, as part of your

116

journey into becoming who you are now. People who hurt other people are usually operating in some type of dysfunction.

Throughout my life, I have never completely fit in with others. Most often, I have been told that I am way too dramatic. I have always thought big and dreamed big, without knowing why I am this way. At one point, I almost convinced myself that my emotions, thoughts, desires, and dreams were unrealistic, until I realized that these were my own natural feelings, so I owned them. Now I purposely live up to them. That was my very own aha moment!

I have removed all those things that could have destroyed me and torn me apart. I decided to learn from them, and in searching for understanding I came to realize that I was a student absorbing everything I could from every situation. I was in the school of life, taught by some of the most powerful teachers—named Trial and Error.

Now the time has come for me to be the instructor, and I'm grateful for that. I do not profess to know everything, for no one does. But I know that we must all be careful not to conform to what other people want us to be. You must walk boldly into your own person and be who God has called you to be. As you grow in this process, you will weed out what is unnecessary for your life, and bring to you what is necessary.

You will also realize that the things that are necessary for your life will benefit the lives of others. Whatever your skill or your talent is, it will benefit someone else. So be the best to yourself that you can be in everything you do. Everything you are is already embedded in you. Follow your dream and your passion, and they will lead you to your purpose. You will find yourself in the most fulfilling place in your life. Remember, if you want a blessing, *be* one.

You know better than anyone else what your purpose is. I may not know you, but I have prayed that everyone who reads this book begins to live purposely on Cloud 9. I know you will, but it is completely up to you. Your time is now.

I believe that you will have the opportunity to share your life in whatever area you choose. If you decide to become a neurosurgeon, you will save lives. If you decide to become a fighter pilot, you will protect country. If you decide to become a prison minister, you will deposit hope into people who sometimes seem hopeless.

Being imprisoned does not necessarily mean that you are behind bars. It's all a state of mind. You can be in prison and be freer than someone on the outside. If you want to change your situation, begin to see it as already changed.

It has been said, how can you help others if you cannot help yourself? Therefore, help yourself first and then help others. It's just like flying on an airplane when the flight attendant tells you to put on an oxygen mask before you help your children or anyone else. You cannot help others with things you know nothing about. But you can help them with things you do know about. So begin there.

You may be in the geometry phase of your life, and not quite ready yet for calculus, but there are other people who are still trying to master fundamental math. We all have someone or something that depends upon us, even if it's only a pet. When you go to your workplace, your co-workers are depending on you to complete your assignments 100 percent. That is how people get promoted.

When you move naturally in your purpose, people will be attracted to your cause. People who need you will come to you almost magically, and those you need will appear also. I have not always realized the positive impact that some of my statements have had on people. But then I began to receive countless grateful messages in my Facebook inbox. One of those messages rings heavy in my heart. It was from a married man who began by telling me how beautiful he thought I was. He said he loved my spirit and would like to have lunch with me. I thanked him for his compliments, but told him that lunch was out of the question. Then I told him how disrespectful he was to me and his wife, even though she probably unaware of what he was doing. Single women who allow themselves to get into situations like this should be prepared for damnation in other areas of their life. It's not a question of *if* damnation is coming, only *when*.

The man wrote more about his wife and the problems they were having. I told him that the best thing he could do would be to begin to work on himself—that he could not change his wife, but he could change himself, and she would observe his change, and hopefully things would get better. The first thing he needed to change was his desire to seek extramarital affairs, because his intentional deceit was only harming himself. Once again, you reap what you sow.

The good news is that, four months later, I received a message from the wife, saying that she wished more women were like me. Prior to her husband writing to me, she said, he had written to other women. But in the last few months, things had changed. She and her husband were no longer having problems, so she was happy that he originally approached me. Soon, she sent me a friend request, and we are now Facebook friends.

Wives depend on their husbands, and husbands depend on their wives. Whether or not your family will be productive depends on how you treat each other. Everyone achieves more when he or she is part of a team.

God gave me the opportunity to speak the right words and serve as an eye-opener to that man, and I'm very grateful I did. I adore watching how their love is blossoming more and more. The husband recently thanked me for helping him to see the greatness that he had right in front of him. I told him that although he was welcome, I did not do it for him or for her. I did it for myself. In the future, when I am married again, and my husband's eyes begin to wander, I pray that he meets a woman just like me.

I have not always thought the way I do now, but today I am purposely focused, and therefore I sow only seeds that I do not mind seeing harvested in my life. I do realize that sometimes love gets stale, but you have to re-create it over and over again.

Love is a beautiful thing, and you must work at it to keep it amazing. So continue to make yourself better in preparation for what God has in store for you. Make every effort to be dependable, and remember to experience God's favor. He has to be able to trust you. Can *you* be trusted?

Chapter 11:

Reflections of Your

Past

Your past created who you are today. What you do with that creation from this point on is up to you. Everything that you have been doing with your life is the very dynamic that makes you *you.*

Do not let anyone else tell you what you are not, when God has already shown you who you are. We have to make mistakes in life because that's how we grow and learn. If we do not make mistakes, we will not have anything to measure success by. The important part of making mistakes is to grow from them and learn from them. It is in your pains that you find your greatest gains. Once you recognize your mistakes, you have opportunities to heal and grow.

Pay attention to relationships of people who have not healed their dysfunctions. When they date others, they generally attract people with the same characteristics over and over again. That is because they never learn their necessary lessons. Unconsciously, you will attract the same types of characters into your life, again and again. The only thing that will change is the faces.

Have you ever noticed how abused women often go from one abusive relationship to the next? You must intentionally recognize the character defects and flaws within yourself that you want to change. That will help you to select a new mate.

Your outlook will naturally determine how you handle situations. For example, if you and I were both drug abusers, hanging out at the park, and someone offered us drugs, our natural reaction would be the excitement and thrill of getting our next high. Now let's flip the story. You and I are doctors, having lunch at the same park, and when someone offers us drugs, we will gather up our belongings and immediately leave, because this is not the environment for us.

Where you are in life determines how you react to everything. Everyone is a product of their environment, whether constructive or destructive. The life you were exposed to, including your geographical location, determines a lot about who you will become. In any case, never despise your past. What can destroy you are the very things that will shape you into the person you need to be. Take care about what you choose to bring into your future from your past. Negative things should be left behind.

The past is behind you. The future is in front of you. Some of the pains of your childhood may have been devastating and debilitating, but until you completely and deliberately make the decision to free yourself from your past, you will not be free. Do not let your past hold you prisoner from your future. Your future will take the pains of your past and turn them into gains that will last.

Do not concern yourself with the thoughts of others and how they may perceive you. If you have to pretend to be someone else in order to be with other people, you should not desire their company in the first place. Be naturally who you are, so that you can attract the people who should be around you. Do not worry about society, or even about impressing friends or parents. None of that matters. Your sanity and a positive opinion of yourself are the most important gifts you can give yourself.

What good would it do you to suppress who you are and live a life that you were not meant to live? You were meant to live your life on purpose and within your purpose. Make it a habit not to talk about painful things in a way that keeps you in bondage. Rather, speak about them from a place of healing. Your story can help others to find their way.

Consider molestation for an example. If you were a molested child who blamed yourself throughout your life, it's time for you to know without a doubt that what happened was not your fault. The benefit of such a terrible occurrence in your life is that you can take this time to reach out to other victims of molestation. That is the opportunity of a lifetime, because you get to reach people where they are hurting and to reassure them that they can live a life without blame. You can protect them from lifelong depression and low self-esteem.

No matter what the traumas in your life may have been, imagine having someone else to travel your journey with and to hear their stories. This will be wonderful, especially if you are lonely, confused, and purposeless. That is why I wrote this book. I lived in that land for a long time, but when I started living purposely on Cloud 9, I couldn't wait to share it with the world.

It is a great feeling when another person understands what you've been through and is willing to help you to see the best in yourself. Just think how much farther along you would be if you had known them sooner.

I know how much farther along I would have been if the proper help had been given to me. I now understand the benefits of paying attention to my own actions, because they cause the reactions of other people and the things that happen to me in my life. I do not regret having had traumatic experiences, because they gave me knowledge that I can share with you. I don't mind being a sacrifice if I can give others aha moments.

Just take the negative things that you experienced in your life and flip them over to become positive. If you were abused, serve in an abuse outreach program. Just keep in mind that there is great richness in everything from your past, even the painful parts. You can take something positive from them that will benefit others. Remember, it's not about you, it's about taking what you've learned and sharing it.

When you are going through your past pains, I'm sure you can recall feeling that they would never end. But they did, didn't they?

Even if you're going through pain right now, you are being given the ability to recognize that everything that happens in your life is a part of who you are. Learn from that.

Sometimes, you may feel that being rejected by another person means that something is defective or wrong in you. What you need to realize is that the rejection is a redirection to bigger and better opportunities. Force yourself to be optimistic. Some people believe that forced optimism is a form of lying. I believe the total opposite. Remained in a low emotional state is a choice. Recognize that, see the situation for what it is, and look for what you are supposed to learn from it. Grow from it and move on.

Even if someone dear to you dies, you must allow yourself the time to grieve, all the while knowing that God is bearing your burdens with you. Appreciate the time you had with your loved one, and turn your tears into positive memories. Give yourself the benefit of knowing your purpose and understanding that your grieving will help to heal you. In fact, that thought will enable you to heal much faster.

You will be so consciously aware of who you are in your purpose that you will know that whatever it is you experience, including the death of loved ones, only makes you stronger. Do not wallow in self-pity, as some people do.

You will learn not only to allow the reflections on your past to benefit you, but to enable you to look forward to the mirrors of your future. You must practice being happy all the time, despite what is going on in your life. Is this easy? No, but it's beneficial to your health. Yes, you will have sad moments, but you will recognize them as simply that: *moments.* And you will not allow yourself to live in that state for very long. It is not good for the body, the mind, or the soul to be unhappy. You have a natural ability to seek and see your happiness. You are now so in tune with your emotional self that if you feel yourself slipping away, simply recognize that and immediately pick yourself up.

Everything is exactly how you perceive it to be. Everything is exactly what you believe it to be. So you have to believe that everything is great. When you do, you will bring greatness and more to yourself. That is God's law.

Chapter 12:
Receiving Your
Transformation

Once you have become intentionally and consciously aware of everything in your life, it will completely change. The very first and most important task to be done is to make sure you're taking care of yourself. In doing that, you have to understand who you are and your purpose.

To begin, you must consciously speak peacefully, even in negative situations. You have to identify the things in life that are sent to distract you from your purpose. If you know that certain things send you over the edge, do not allow them to do that. Consciously change your reaction.

People will notice your change. Some may question your sincerity, but, again, the opinions of others do not matter. You must live your life on purpose. That does not mean you will be Mr. or Mrs. perfect each and every day. Rather, it means that you have recognized all of these things within yourself, and that gives you the ability to teach others how to do it. It also means that you will continue to develop yourself. But do not think that you have the ability to change others, because you don't. God is the only one with that power. But what he does is place you in the lives of other people to inspire them to change. Sometimes that means loving them unconditionally, so that they can see the love of God through you.

When a person is ready to change, there is nothing that can stop that change because it motivated by desire. On the other hand, when a person tries to change to accommodate someone else, the change is short-lived.

If a person has never tasted a certain food, he or she may or may not like it. However, sometimes it is an acquired taste. But once the acquisition is complete, it can become a desired taste. This describes my newfound love affair with sushi. I remember a time when you could not get me to taste it. When I tried it the first time, I hated it.

The next time I tried it, I was on a date, and the man ordered it for me. That time, the sushi was magnificent. Now I eat it all the time. My date did not make me like sushi, but he introduced it to me in such a way that it is now one of my favorite foods.

But what you accept or reject is still up to you. Just as you can't change anyone else, neither can anyone else change you. You must be inspired to transform from within. The pain that you consider the most impactful in your life will also be the pain that empowers you to live up to your full purpose. You just have to make sure that the pain is a lesson that you learn, and not allow it to debilitate you and keep you isolated. Learn from your pain, and then you can release it. You have to know that things happen in life that you will have no control over. The inability to change some of those situations can leave you in a vulnerable state of confusion, loneliness, and emptiness. The simplest and most fulfilling way to get past those emotions is to always perceive pain as fuel for your purpose.

That makes pain extremely worthwhile. If you cannot change a situation, make the best of it. Consciously adjust your stress meter by purposely seeing the positive in life and disregarding the negative. Your life will adapt to this change. Because you will be able to do this, you won't have low lows, but you will have extremely amazing highs, which will catapult you up to Cloud 9, giving you the ability to maintain your life up there.

Life is going to happen, whether you are part of it or not. There will be good times and bad. But who says the bad times are really bad. You give meaning to what is good or bad. So embrace the bad times to learn from them. You will have great times in life, and others that are not so great, but in either case you must have an innate sense of peace and understanding, knowing that everything is exactly how it should be right now. Whatever it is that you are experiencing is going to be a part of your history. So it's up to you how you process "the right now," and part of that is knowing that everything is purposed. Even more important, everything is going to be alright.

Storms do come, and sometimes they bring terrible lightning, but you have been equipped with an emotional umbrella that protects you. Although it's raining hell all around you, you are covered.

Sometimes, it may seem that things are bad and getting worse, but due to your wisdom and your understanding of life and its purpose, you know that it's all a part of the process. It's all about perception.

In the midst of turmoil, find something positive to focus on. Positivity is the key to being released and relieved from all stresses and pains in this world. There is no negative in positive. So when life seems to pull you down, your intentional, purposeful living will give you what I like to call the rubber band effect, which is the ability to bounce back from any and all situations while still maintaining your form.

I'm sure there are situations in which you feel that you have not done your best. Or you may even think you failed. We all have such moments, so do not beat yourself up over them. Your past is just your past. People will sometimes try to rub your nose in it, but don't allow that to cause you to lose focus. If they are still living in the past, that is their choice. That was then, and this is now. You have moved, and your past is no longer your address.

You may not be doing exactly what you want to do in life, but the mere fact that you are reading this book shows that you are looking for ways to empower yourself and to make changes. You are taking the necessary steps to make amazing things happen in your life. You have purpose on this Earth, or you wouldn't be here. That is a fact. I'm sure that you do not want to end up in the land of regret. That is a very lonely place, and everyone there is sad.

The difference between you and them is that you now have the power to make anything happen that you want. Just go for it, letting nothing and no one hold you back. The sky is not the limit, for you can reach beyond this dimension. You can do anything you want. You just have to believe it to be true.

There will be people who laugh at and ridicule your newfound optimism. Many will simply not believe you, or believe *in* you. But you cannot let those people stop you. If you have a dream and a vision, continue pushing it, even when you feel as though you are the only pusher.

Trust and believe me, the God of the universe is pushing with you, too. If you are already living the life of your dreams, and operating in your purpose, congratulations to you. May you continue to be blessed and a blessing to others. Please continue to help make dreams come true for others.

If you have not yet found your purpose or your meaning, the first thing you must do is truly desire change. You must adopt a new way of thinking, a new focus, and possibly even a new geographical location. Listen to the quiet voice that lives inside you. Pay attention to the desires that live in you. Focus on your visions and bring them to life. There should no longer be a day of unfulfillment. You are the author of your thoughts. If they have entered your mind, then you have the power to bring them to fruition. You are now ready to place one foot in front of the other. You may not know exactly where you're going, or even how to get there. But what you do know is that you are walking in your purpose, and your purpose will lead you to your destiny. You cannot concentrate on what you do not have, or on obstacles that you foresee. You are moving in your purpose, and your purpose will make way for you.

You start by being absolutely grateful for everything in your life. Being intentionally grateful will definitely instantly manifest more things to be grateful for. True joy does not come from tangible things, but from knowing who you are and what your purpose is. Then everything else will fall into place. What you cannot do is give too much focus to the negative things that people say. Your purpose is inside you, God gave you your vision. If others do not see what you see, don't let their lack of vision cause you to go blind.

Dreaming your vision is just like dreaming when you are asleep.

You are the one who is sleeping and dreaming. No one can sleep or dream for you, just as no one can live your Life for you. God gave you the dream. He will also give you the team to make it happen. But be prepared for not everyone on your team being a team player. Even Jesus had a Judas. And just like Jesus, you do not have to call out your foes individually. You can let them know that you are aware of what they are up to, just as Jesus informed his apostles at the last supper. He knew exactly who would do what, but he washed their feet anyway.

Even when people are cruel to you if God has given you an assignment in their life, follow through, for God does not change his mind. We do, and in doing so we block our very own blessings that God has designed for us. You can and will receive those blessings whenever you complete God's assignments. But just like any other tests, you don't have to continue to take them if you pass the first time.

Criticism can sometimes be very constructive. It will teach you to perfect your craft. Do not let it break you, but only strengthen you. Do not give in to negativity. But you should not completely ignore criticism, for it can be an excellent measure. Negative criticism does not have to cause you to stop and change your direction if that's not what you desire. What it should trigger you to do is pay attention to what you're doing, and if you're on the right track, then who cares? If you see room for improvement, you get the opportunity to make the necessary corrections.

Do not let your emotions make life-changing decisions for you. Decisions based on emotions alone are usually disastrous. You must understand that everyone has a right to his or her own opinion. That's why it's called an opinion. Everyone has one. In most cases, it doesn't determine who's right or wrong. It's just two different people's different perspectives. Adults should be able to agree to disagree.

What you are responsible for is being the best you that you can be in all that you do. Take control of yourself when the approval of others is nonexistent. Life around you is absolutely amazing. And you have intentionally focused on the things that are amazing. View the world as beautiful as it is. God gave us this beautiful planet and everything on it. We only have a short time to be here, so why not make the best of your stay?

When you're driving past buildings, street signs, and other cars, be grateful that you have the ability to see these things, because everyone does not have sight. If there is something you desire, and you see that someone else has received it, do not become disgusted or feel that you will never obtain or achieve it. Do not become envious. Jealousy is the root of all evil. Evil is negativity, so you have just blocked your blessings. Instead, realize that you being around to see another person receive a blessing is proof that God is bringing the blessing closer to you. When you respect and appreciate others being blessed, you open up the gateway of blessings for yourself.

Consciously being positive and surrounding yourself with positive people produces positive results. Living in this land of intentional positivity will make you feel focused, as if you could fly. Will you slip emotionally while living on Cloud 9? Absolutely. But because of your ability to recognize your emotions clearly, you will intentionally return yourself to Cloud 9 immediately. There is no place else that you would rather be than happy, hopeful, positive, and purposed. Applying positivity every day will become a natural habit—and what better habit could you have?

You have exposed yourself to such a wonderful state of mind, which no amount of money can purchase. You now know how wonderful it is and how fantastic it feels to be consciously happy and on purpose every day. Who wouldn't want to return immediately to Cloud 9? You have witnessed the joy of living on Cloud 9, so you know how to appreciate every person who comes into your life. You are aware that that people have reasons, seasons, and sometimes lifetime positions in your life. You will have the ability to respect every single one of them for their purpose.

As time passes, and you have the ability to reflect, you understand your purpose more and more clearly. What it is doing is making a way for you to recognize and appreciate your lifetime seasons better. You are entitled to joy, because happiness is fleeting, but joy is internal and eternal—it is *yours*. No one can take it from you. Only you can give it away. In this transformation, you must transform your mind. It is the way you think and the way you perceive all things that determines the emotions you connect to it.

Pay attention to people who think and talk negatively about others. These are usually negative people themselves. When you begin to feel a sloping in your spirit, check your surroundings and the type of people you are allowing into your space. No one can get into your space unless you open the door for them.

Just because things may not go exactly as you thought they should does not mean that you are not on purpose. Living purposefully does not come without opposition. You just handle it differently. It actually may bring even more distractions to challenge you, so be prepared. Recognize the deceivers for exactly who they are. Will those things that are coming to distract you be hideous, so that you can recognize the monster? Absolutely not. It will be everything that appears perfect. Remember, Satan has many disguises. He is a tempter, whose job is to kill, steal, and destroy. He will package temptation perfectly for your destruction, unless you recognize it because of your ability to discern.

Discernment gives you the ability to see through deception, enabling you to redirect your focus. Most importantly, in transforming your life and the way you think, what you need to guard the most is your mind. Whatever has control of your mind also has control of your time as well as your life. Be careful where you spend it. Be sure to condition your mind to think the thoughts you want to think. If you allow negative thoughts to consume your mind, they will pull you in and have your mind racing. That is how people lose their minds. Do not let your mind control you. You must control it. You are in control of your own thoughts; your thoughts must not be in control of you.

Just as you communicate with people, you can communicate with your own mind. Speak to your mind and tell it how you want to feel. For example, tell yourself, "I am happy. I am hopeful. I am excited." Whatever you say will manifest life. There is death and life in the power of the tongue.

Whatever you speak, you shall have. Some things may not happen instantly, but you spoke them; therefore, believe that they will come. Do not give in to doubt, even in frivolous situations. Do not say that you knew something unfortunate was going to happen. The keyword is *knew*. Because you thought it, you felt it, and therefore it happened. Expect the best all the time. If something does happen that does not go the way you expected, it is not your fault. You did your part; let life do its part. Just allow life to happen, and be still in your mind and in your spirit.

Having your new level of consciousness does not make you immune to emotions. Sometimes, you might have to take a moment to stop and breathe. If you have to cry, cry! But I promise, it will be a new cry for you, and one with purpose. Since you understand your purpose, even your tears have new meaning.

I can recall times when my financial situation was not so good. It almost made me feel that I couldn't speak about purpose and what purpose brings if I was suffering in that area. But what I realized was that, even in the midst of a financial struggle, I was not depleted. In fact, I was more on purpose than ever. I just continued to walk by faith and belief. New opportunities and possibilities continued to occur almost instantly. People whom I didn't even know called with blessings for me—not just for me personally, but also for my girls foundation.

So do your best, and let God do the rest. Don't give up on life, and life won't give up on you.

Chapter 13:

You Are Now Purposely

Living on Cloud 9

Wow, oh wow! Welcome to Cloud 9! I'm so glad to finally see you here. This is a place where, once you have arrived, you do everything in your power to stay. By the end of this chapter, you will know how to stay here forever.

You don't accidentally arrive at Cloud 9. Occasionally, people get close, but in order to maintain residence, everything is intentional. You have to pay attention to the choices you make to maintain your life on Cloud 9. Living on Cloud 9 does not mean that every day is going to be perfect. You must be aware that even when things are not going great, that does not mean you are no longer on

Cloud 9. It only means that you have temporarily lost your footing because you were slightly distracted.

Because of your keen sense of purpose, you now have the ability to return yourself to Cloud 9 at the drop of a dime. In your daily communication with people, make sure that you listen to every conversation with a keen sense of how you can help to make situations better. When someone speaks to you about negative things they are going through, that is God opening the door to test your positive outlook on life. If God did not want you to let his light shine through you, he would not have exposed you to the conversation. Even if the conversation is not directed to you, if you are allowed to hear it, it does not necessarily mean that you are to become a Butt-in-ski. What you should do is immediately begin to pray for what you have heard.

Sometimes a conversation that you have overheard may be something that you've spoken to God about in your prayer or meditation. This conversation could serve as the necessary confirmation that you needed.

Almost 100 percent of the time when someone asks me how I am doing, I respond that I am superfantastic, and getting better by the second. This usually catches people off guard, because they are used to hearing the typical "I'm good. And you?" But life for you is no longer good, it is great. It is fantastic. It is splendid.

What this does for the person you're responding to is instantly jar their thought process. They may not know that you are on Cloud 9, but you do, and they will wonder why you feel so fantastic. It is your opportunity to spread the joy of living on Cloud 9 to everyone you come into contact with. When I first arrived on Cloud 9, I experienced an amazing high. It felt so good that I not only knew that I wanted to stay there forever, but I also noticed that there weren't many people there at any one time.

Many people tried to convince me that this state of being was temporary. When I first heard those words, I have to admit that I was unnerved a little. I immediately began to think about life before my Cloud 9 state of living. I had often experienced pleasant times in my life, but nothing that could be compared to being on Cloud 9. It made me wonder if this was just an illusion.

That was one of the saddest feelings I can ever remember having. What would I do if this amazing feeling left me? But a year and a half later, I am *still* high. And I'm not coming down!

I have trained myself to focus on only the good things in life. Whenever I feel the slightest negativity, I intentionally find something good to say. I think about what I'm giving to others, and what I will receive back. I do not want to bring any negativity to myself. I think of it as taking a hammer and driving a nail through my own toe. It would cripple me, not the other person.

So what I had to do was figure out how to introduce this amazing feeling to the entire world. What good is it to live here on Cloud 9 all by myself? I had to figure out a way to help people turn their lives into a perpetual state of joy. I had to figure out what was missing in the lives of so many people that the entire world did not live in a state of bliss. Your situation does not make you. You make your situation. It doesn't matter how much money you have in the bank or where you live. You can still be miserable with a lot of money. Once you begin to live purposely on Cloud 9, you will forever exist in a natural state of euphoria.

What I had to learn is that some people enjoy functioning in their dysfunction. Not everyone wants to be happy. Some people are natural mess magnets. When you are exposed to people like that, even when they don't recognize this character defect in themselves,

147

immediately pray for them, and make sure you do not allow their thinking to corrupt your journey.

I decided to share my story with so many people, and they would see how elated I was with life despite my humble circumstances. They would instantly begin to thank me for sharing my story, as well as for the encouraging words I would have for them. More and more people began to lean on me, and as much as I appreciated it, it began to become extremely time-consuming. So I had to figure out how to get the word out without that problem. And immediately I felt in my spirit that I had to write about it.

That is how and why this book was born. My plan is to get the world high, one book at a time. Everyone deserves peace of mind and a sense of purpose. And until you arrive at that point in your life, you will never be comfortable.

I experienced several losses as I was writing this book, including the deaths of several loved ones. That was painful and devastating, but I understood that there was still purpose. God is still God, and God is still good. I hope this book will continue to add to your life and the lives of everyone you tell about it. I am eternally grateful to be responsible for the positive impact on the world that this book will bring. It is my gift to the world, and I am grateful for everything that has happened to me. You must be grateful for everything that has happened to you.

One thing that has kept me throughout my life is the significance of the number 3. My initials were triple *B*'s. Threes also meant that God's eyes were on me. Even as a kid when I saw a 3, I knew God could see me. It has always been my favorite number for many reasons, but primarily because of the Father, the Son, and the Holy Ghost. Creation begins with a threesome: a male, a female, and a baby. It's just the cycle of life. You are born, you live, and you die. So why not live your life intentionally high on everything positive that life is giving you?

Three is so significant to me that every time I see it, no matter where, it signifies to me that God is still thinking of me. If there is a confirmation of anything that I need, I believe that God sends signs to me, and he uses the number three often in my life. Whatever emotion I'm in, when I see the number 3, I pay attention. If I'm feeling happy, I appreciate that feeling. If I have slipped into a slumber, it is a reminder that I'm slipping. Whatever I'm experiencing, the number 3 causes me to focus. It is my absolute favorite number.

Call me silly if you must, but when I see a 3 I get excited, like a kid who has just received candy. I suggest that you pick something that *you* love to remind you to pay attention. Make sure it's something that you see often. It should remind you of the greatness of the world, as well as the greatness within you, for you are on Cloud 9. You are on purpose. Doesn't it feel great? Isn't it a wonderful place to be? I'm excited for you that you're here. I look forward to you discovering the new you.

That is a daily process, which must be practiced intentionally. The good news is that you have taken the opportunity. The bad news is that there will be some people who read this book and view it as just another book. That is fine, for you have been exposed to its good news. Now you know where to find it. Whenever you're ready, you can pick this book up again, and it will be right there to give you all you need, and all you're willing to receive.

To those of you who are ready to live your life purposefully till the end, if you're feeling anything like I do, please know that you do not ever have to come down. You can stay high if you try. The best thing that ever happened to me was to understand how to intentionally stay on Cloud 9. I'm so glad that I mastered that, and I'm even more excited to share these instructions with you. I look forward to hearing your stories. There is no such thing as overcrowding on Cloud 9. I also look forward to the world reflecting the positive changes in life that are necessary to give people the completion to their existence on Earth.

There is far more to life than materialistic things. You have earned the right to be happy and full of joy. You can now understand that whatever it is you go through, there was a purpose in it for you. You cannot measure yourself by anything anyone else says or does. Your life is yours, and only yours.

To maintain this state of being is truly up to you. Whether you remain on Cloud 9 is up to you. If you choose to allow your surroundings to change your focus, you have no one to blame but yourself. I refuse to be removed from Cloud 9, and I ask you to refuse as well. I cannot wait to see and hear and read about all of the transformations that have come about in you from reading this book—how everything in you came alive: businesses, ministries, children, families, relationships, love, and the ability to be who you are completely and wholly.

That is why there is now a website for all of your testimonials. Please come and talk to me. I look forward to hearing from you. I will do my best to respond to every single one of you, because you matter to me. I am praying for you, your family, and your dreams. May your wounds be healed so that you are restored in every area where you need restoration. I cannot wait to see you on the website:

PurposelyLivingOnCloud9.com

Keep in mind that we are all here to serve. What we must do is understand that one principle of life, and everything else will fall into place. Everyone must become a giver. The beautiful part of giving is that you bring someone else joy and happiness.

It is a fact that happy people who have tapped into this have begun to live longer, stronger, healthier lives. Giving is the best thing other than receiving. It also increases your life. It is very important that you participate in selfless service. Not only do you help yourself, but you help others. In doing so, you will see transformations in your own life that you never expected . You do not give with an expectation of receiving, but the joy of giving is that the law naturally gives back to you. Going outside yourself and helping the world is much bigger than money when you totally understand. You realize that you have given yourself away, and in doing that you can take control and power into your hands by helping others in ways you never imagined.

But be careful how you use this power, because if it's misappropriated, it will be removed just as quickly as it was given. You will have developed a happiness that cannot be removed. The selfish self has been replaced with your purposed self. You are now living blissfully, purposely, and intentionally, and you have the ability to bring others with you. Whatever you are responsible for will come back to you.

If you give the toll-taker at the bridge something to smile about, he or she will pass on the same joy to the next driver, and that person will pass it on to someone else. Thus, you are not only responsible for the joy of one individual, but of many. So, when you give joy and happiness intentionally, all of that will be returned to you in far greater measure than you can ever imagine. Be very careful what you are passing on, because negativity can be spread in the same way. Be responsible for doing great things. Be responsible for contributing joy and greatness to the world.

My challenge to you is to have a giving party. Whether you have it in your home or church, make sure that giving is always the primary focus. People feel so good when things are given to them. You make a natural lasting impression on their minds and hearts, so when they want to give to others, you will probably be the first person they think of, because you assisted in opening their minds, and gave their lives new meaning. God will so align your life that, in one form or fashion, your giving will be reciprocated.

There are so many things in this world that we take for granted every day. If you decide to seek shade under a tree, chances are that you didn't plant that tree, but you are reaping its benefits. It works the same way when you give to others without any expectation of receiving back from them. What you gave may not come from the same place, but it does come from someplace.

Another thing you must pass on is the gift of being grateful. When you are grateful for whatever it is you have, you bring more of what you want into your life. You must always find reasons to be grateful. If you own an old car, be grateful that you have one at all, and don't have to walk everywhere. If you are a paraplegic, be grateful that you are alive. Even if you have been diagnosed as terminally ill, believe that things can change and they will. Even when your loved ones die, just be grateful for the time you had with them, for it was longer than the time someone else had on this planet.

I make it a focus point to teach gratitude to the girls of GyyC. One of the gratitude exercises that I do with them is ask them to close their eyes, and imagine being blind. I instruct them very sternly not to open their eyes until they hear the exact words "Open your eyes." With their eyes closed, I take them through the daily processes of waking up, getting dressed, brushing and combing their hair, having breakfast, going to school, participating in school activities, and returning home. Then I ask them to open their eyes and be grateful that they can see, because someone somewhere cannot.

Another gratitude exercise they do involves asking them to hold their hands behind their backs, and they cannot release their hands until they hear the exact words, "Release your hands." I then tell them to brush their hair, scratch their cheek, tie their shoes, write their names, and many other things that require hands. When I ask them to release their hands, they are so grateful that they have eyes, arms, and hands to do things with. This instills gratitude at a very early age.

The most important thing you need to know and hold near and dear to your heart as you continue your Cloud 9 living is that, in all things good, you have God! Even if you are an atheist, God still lives in *good*. Because God is good. There is no way around it. And God is so amazing that he loves unbelievers just as much as believers. God is love. So whatever you love, you are showing the spirit of God intentionally or unintentionally. Wherever there is love, there is God, because God first loved you. For God so loved that he gave. Remember, *love* is an action word. The key to Cloud 9 living is giving. No matter what you give, just give. Continue to give for the rest of your life, and you will receive for lifetime.

3 things to remember:

- BE GRATEFUL ALL THE TIME! Gratitude is the KEY to Living a Purposed Life!!!
- Repeat your Personal Decree every day. Tear it out and post it somewhere that you can see it often.
- Life is all about perception. However you perceive anything to be, then *it is*.

*** PERSONAL DECREE***

I am amazing. I am loved. It doesn't matter who loves me. I love me. I'm confident in who I am. I choose to live my life on purpose. I understand that this may not be easy, but I refuse to give up. I will fight for me and for you. I believe in us. We can do all things and anything that we put our minds to do. All goals are achievable. All unhealthy dysfunctions are removed. I am free regardless of who likes me. I will not be defined by others. I will be who I was purposed to be. And that is me. I will walk with my head high, even when the masses do not agree. I will stand for what I believe. I believe in me. Together we can and will live our life purposely on Cloud 9.

Acknowledgments

My first and most important thank you is to God. Thank you for my yesterdays. Thank you for my today. Thank you for my tomorrows. It is because in you I live. Thank you for choosing me. I am grateful that I have sense enough to choose you as well. Wherever my road leads me in whatever condition, you will be sending me. I will *go*, because I know I am not alone, for you are with me. Amen.

Thank you to Bishop Thomas Dexter Jakes for allowing God to use you in such a mighty way for millions of people. Every time you speak, I hear the voice of God speaking through you directly to me. Thank you also, First Lady Serita Jakes, for being the spine in the Bishop's back. I can only imagine the strength you must have. Thank you, First Family, for sharing your father with the people. I can only imagine the tug of war.

Thank you, Paul Weisser, for being an amazing editor. You took time with me to make sure that this book has a voice of its own. Not only did you bring this book to life, but you made sure that every word would be understood by everyone.

Thank you to my biological sons: Jazz, I am so grateful that your birth saved my life. My apologies to you for everything that I did not know as I was raising you. But I did the best I could with what I knew then. And I've taken what I've learned and shared it with the world. I love you so much, son, and thank you for loving me just as much. You have a heart of gold, and it is exciting to watch you come into your own.

Chandler, I am often in awe at how much you remind me of *me*. You are a dreamer and a go-getter. Recognize that the enemy is busy and will set up traps, so don't fall in. Continue to be the leader that you are, and the kind of follower you would want to lead. I also love you so much, son, and thank you for loving me just as much, too.

Thank you to my nonbiological children: Shakaria, Martinay, and M.J., the three of you added to the fabric of who I am. I'm glad that God allowed me to share a part of your life. You guys are all parents now. Please be the best parents you can be. I love you all very much.

Marcus Stern, my former husband, I'm very grateful for the fourteen years we shared. It was a very necessary chapter in my life. I consider it the cocoon phase of my life. Thank you for that time, it played a major role in me becoming the Butterfly I am today. I wish you nothing but joy, happiness, and peace for the rest of your life. No longer my husband, Forever my friend.

Roslyn Wiley, thank you for teaching me how to give without expectation. You planted seeds in the unknown, but I hope you see what they've blossomed into. You were the windowpane in my life. Without you I would be shattered glass. You rule with an iron fist, but that was very necessary for the wild child that I was. Thank you for that, and I love you even more for it. You were like a mommy, a sister, and a best friend when I needed all three.

Wilbernita Sue Kinney-Crosby (also known as Sue Cool), thank you so much for being the woman of God that you are, and the wind beneath my wings. Your spirit of excellence, your ability to dream, your great expectations, and your support are all things that I needed. Thank you for allowing God to use you in my life. I see myself in you so much. If my mother were here, I would wish that she were just like you. I love you, mommy (in my Tooti-voice)

Anissa Michelle, where do I start? *Thank you* really says it all, but let me be a little more specific. You have been my cousin, my best friend, my sister, my confidante, and my angel. I'm so grateful that our parents are brother and sister, for that created the original bond. But our commonalities created the lifetime connection. My instructions about you from God were, "She was there for you in your Mess; you must remember that in your Bless." The good news is, I'm grateful to follow those orders, and wouldn't have it any other way.

There are so many other family members, friends, and even people who have thought of themselves as my enemies, who have added to the fabric of my being. Nothing that anyone has ever done for me is

160

unappreciated. I am very grateful to the countless numbers of you, whose names would fill pages. Thank for seeding into my life. For we are nothing without the help of others.

So let me say collectively, thank you, *everyone*, for all that you are and have been in my life. Each and every one of you has played an intricate part in the process of who I am. I am grateful beyond measure.

This part right here is for my Kickstarters

The people listed below supported this book through a website that supports projects large and small. Thank you all for believing in my project enough to become a backer. I am forever indebted to each and every one of you, for you are the primary reason this book exists. Together we will provide the information within these pages, hoping that the necessary transformations occur every minute of the day.

Mae Grigsby, better known as my Aunt Diddy, thank you, Aunti, for loving me so much and always seeing the best in me. Thank you for not only telling me that your house is always my home, but for showing me that as well. Thank you for being the driving force behind the Kickstart campaign. I am forever grateful, and love you so much.

Below are the Kickstarters who backed this project:

Andrea Johnson
Kay Williams
Jenifer Jackson
Charles Bacy Jr.
Keisha Hurd-Bacy
Andy Brown
Maurice Anderson
Akita and Trina Graves
Edwin Konger
Reginald Morris Sr.
Sielio Butler
Harold Slack
R. Richards, II
Mattie Hardin
Derrick Lagrone
Melody
Shanna Scott
Ingrid Thompson
Anissa Mills
Jazz Johnson
Tracie Wright
Saundra McDowell
Glenn Smith
Kisha McDonald
Rhonda Hudson
Marilynn Lightner
Vanessa Gipson
Cynthia Plummer
Mae Grigsby
Malcolm Finkley
Jevette Bacy
LaVonda Sterns-Bacy
Candace Collins
Mary
Pee Wee
Khrislyn
Tikina Lewis
Wilbernita Crosby
Cedrick Harris

Gerald Piper
Julie Legler
Vanessa Washington
Bernard Porter
Jordana Hoffman
Colecia Williams
Theresa Mitchell
Beverly Johnson
E. J. Bacy
Nicole Peters
Kimberly Mitchell
Bridget Williams
Michael Caesar
Regina Fuller
Bianca McCloud
Clifford Fuller
Nicole Todd
Paulett McCowan
Michelle Johnson
Teresa Ackerson

NOTES

www.ingramcontent.com/pod-product-compliance
Lightning Source LLC
LaVergne TN
LVHW022340080426
835508LV00012BA/1291